WHAT WILL WE DO?

Preparing a School Community to Cope with Crises

Editor
Robert G. Stevenson
River Dell Regional Schools
Oradell, New Jersey

Death, Value and Meaning Series
Series Editor: **John D. Morgan**

Baywood Publishing Company, Inc.
AMITYVILLE, NEW YORK

Library of Congress Catalog Number: 94-5217
ISBN: 0-89503-151-5 (Cloth)
ISBN: 0-89503-152-3 (Paper)

Library of Congress Cataloging-in-Publication Data

What will we do? : preparing a school community to cope with crises / editor, Robert G. Stevenson.
p. cm. - - (Death, value, and meaning series)
Includes index.
ISBN 0-89503-151-5. - - ISBN 0-89503-152-3 (pbk.)
1. School psychology- -United States. 2. Crisis management- -United States. 3. Educational counseling- -United States. 4. Crisis intervention (Psychiatry)- -United States. I. Stevenson, Robert G. II. Series.
LB1027.55.W42 1994
371.4'6'0973- -dc20 94-5217
CIP

DEDICATION

This book is dedicated to my family,
my wife Eileen and my sons Robert and Sean
who have supported me in good times and in crises;
my parents Robert and Maura,
my in-laws Dan and Kay and
my surrogate parents Pat and Claire;
and to the students and staff of River Dell High School
who have been a part of our extended family
for almost twenty-five years.

Table of Contents

Introduction

Robert G. Stevenson

Adults see childhood as a time of growth and learning which should be filled with love and joy. In an effort to maintain this ideal image of childhood, it has long been true that adults try to shield children from the emotional pain and turmoil which can intrude upon their lives at any time. In a utopian setting, where such protection might be possible, this task would be well worth the effort. However, the world in which we live today sees children, their families and, at times, their entire communities beset by almost daily crises. If we cannot shield children from the intrusion of such crises, with their accompanying emotional pain and confusion, it might be more effective if we directed our efforts instead at preparing for possible crises and developing resources to assist children to cope with them when they do occur.

Life can be a harsh taskmaster. The lessons our children will learn may be made easier if they can count on assistance from all of the caring adults in their lives. The "devil theory" of history shows us a pattern of reactive behavior in which one person or group is assigned the blame for some historical event or complex social issue. Critics who adhere to a modern "devil theory" in society are quick to assign "blame" to teachers, schools, or social minorities for most of the difficulties encountered by today's students. Phyllis Schlafly and her Eagle Forum have come to represent just such a position. They identify many of the ills in society, often quite correctly, but then see those who try to assist young people to address these problems as the "cause" of the problems. Parents are warned to "investigate" what teachers are doing and these "critics" see the weakening of parental influence and the undermining of family values as goals of educators. Such divisive tactics may appear to address problems, but often only serve as a way to avoid real issues which defy quick or easy solutions.

Should parents be aware of what goes on in a child's classroom? Absolutely! They should know this so that they can work with educators for their child's benefit. Columnist Clarence Page, in a column entitled "When Parents Fail To Do Their Job," (*The Record,* February 1993) agrees with Ms. Schlafly that parents should be involved in their children's lives and does not believe that a school has the right to usurp parental authority. However, "the bigger problem is that some families do such an inadequate job that the community must step in for the sake of the child and the community on the whole. The appalling stream of child-abuse stories shows with grisly clarity that parents don't always know better than the community what's best for their kids. Sometimes parents need help."

There are those who label individuals and then base their reaction to ideas proposed by the individuals on those same labels. Using a label applied to its presenter, or one of that person's roles, as a way to judge the merit of an idea or a program happens far too frequently. This is a quick but often inaccurate way to determine the merit of an idea or program. Each of us plays many roles, as Shakespeare pointed out, and we can be described with any of a number of labels. Allow me to illustrate by using myself as an example. I am a teacher, a counselor and a parent. As a teacher I see young people who believe they are never responsible for consequences of their actions and I resent enabling behavior on the part of counselors and administrators that encourages this personal irresponsibility on the part of students. As a counselor, I see young people who face major crises in their lives which at times must take priority over homework or other academic issues and which should be acknowledged by teachers. As a parent I want to know what is going in the lives of my children and I want only the *best* teachers and the *best* counselors to work with them. Each of these roles is different but they are *not,* as Ms. Schlafly and others would have us believe, adversarial. In each of these roles there is the underlying belief that it is the best interest of the child/student that must take priority and that all other issues are secondary. It would be easy to label me as a conservative, or liberal, with any of the labels that accompany each of my various roles, those listed here or others. To do that is to fail to judge the ideas I present on their merits. The authors whose works are included in this volume have worked through personal losses, accidents and, in one case, major surgery to assemble the book you now hold. They did so not for personal profit, but to present ideas and programs which they believe can help young people, their families, and their schools.

This book is offered as a guide to assist caring adults, both educators and parents, who wish to understand the impact of crises on our children. It also discusses programs which utilize prior planning, education, and identification of sources of support to assist the children who must face such crises. These programs have been shown to meet some of the needs of young people. Their methods are still evolving and can use involvement from all parts of the academic community: parents, teachers, counselors, coaches, administrators, and the students themselves. Sometimes it is not just parents, but all of us, that need help. When the goal is to help our children, people who would divide a community of caring adults do not do the children a service. United, the members of a community can be a strong asset in the lives of the children. In the past there may have been errors of judgement when actions were taken or not taken in response to a particular problem. The goal of this work is *not* to assess blame, it *is* to assist in solving the problem. In helping our schools assist children who face crises the authors of the chapters that follow would agree with Mr. Page's observation that, "the question is not *whether* the community should intervene, it is *when*." With the crises facing today's children, when is *now*.

In the opening chapter of this book, Robert Stevenson presents an overview of the situation. Needs of the students and staff, effects of a crisis on a school and on its students, and the possible benefits of prior preparation are discussed. Margaret Metzgar discusses methods of preparing a school community for crises. She focuses on the role of the steering committee as the key group in establishing a carefully planned, effective district policy for coping with crises. David Meagher also presents a plan for school preparation but focuses on the preparation of staff and, in particular, the Crisis (Response) Team. Eileen Stevenson speaks about the specific role of the school nurse in preparing for crises and as a key medical support person during and after crises. Rabbi Daniel A. Roberts offers a model for religious schools. He presents a model developed in Jewish religious schools, but it is clearly one which moves beyond possible sectarian boundaries and which can be appropriately modified and used in most religious schools.

Special issues also receive attention from the contributors. Diane Ryerson and John Kalafat speak to the crises related to the issue of suicide. They discuss the three aspects of prevention, intervention and postvention in school-based programs. Patricia Zalaznik discusses the modern health crises of HIV/AIDS and their impact on today's students and schools. Violence in schools and surrounding communities is discussed by William Lee, Jr. He believes that any response by schools to this crisis must place violence in context, realizing that in violence there are many victims. He offers guidelines for schools which operate from this basic principle. Linda Reed Maxwell has lived through the crisis which a military family endures in a time of national crisis. Children of these families have special needs as do schools seeking to help these children and their families. Her chapter offers school guidelines for helping children during a time of military crisis.

Sandra Elder conducts a support group for bereaved teens. Her chapter offers guidelines for such support groups and discusses several active groups. Support is needed for all those effected by a crisis, including those who offer support. The Critical Incident Stress Debriefing model is presented in a form which can be utilized in the schools.

Teens can also offer support in times of crises. Robert Stevenson discusses the potential of a peer "Listening" program.

The final section of the book offers answers to questions which have been asked about topics and themes in this book. The crisis section offers a quick, basic reference for use in emergencies when time is an issue and there may not have been sufficient preparation for an immediate crisis or emergency.

If there is one theme which appears in the work of every contributor to this book it is that the time for planning and for action is *now*. The issues discussed here impact schools regularly and a school which does not plan ahead for crises leaves its students and staff at risk while it seeks to react to crisis during or after the fact. It is toward this goal of prior planning that this book is dedicated.

CHAPTER 1

Schools and Crises

Robert G. Stevenson

It is the belief of this author that the crises which exist in each of our lives pose questions which we are called upon to answer. In order to answer these questions effectively, the first question which must be answered is: "What is a crisis?"

Dictionaries define "crisis" in any of several ways. A crisis can be defined as:

- a serious or decisive state of things;
- a turning point when a situation must soon terminate or suffer a material change;
- a decisive or crucial time, stage or event;
- a situation whose outcome will decide whether possible bad consequences will follow;
- in medicine, a turning point which indicates recovery or death.

The emotional health and physical safety of our children are clearly issues that are both serious and decisive. Childhood and adolescence are literally filled with turning points which mark endings and change as children develop into mature adults. Piaget and his successors have shown us that the development of children progresses through stages which provide the foundation for future development. If events which confront a child during these stages of development are not mastered successfully, then "bad consequences" may follow. However, the medical definition may well be the one most used in discussing crises in the lives of our children which involve our schools. The school community must act in ways which will aid recovery if we are to avoid the "death" of academic learning, of emotional growth, of personal potential, of optimism and "dreams."

There is one more definition which must be added. On the most basic level, an event, situation, circumstance is a crisis *if we believe it is*. A track coach was once asked how fast someone had to be moving to be considered "running" (as opposed to jogging). He replied you are moving fast enough to be running any time you believe you are . . . elapsed time has little meaning. On that same level, we are experiencing a crisis any time we believe we are. The labels we apply to an event or the feelings we experience connected to that event may well be the most important factor in determining whether or not an event is a "crisis." With less experience of significant life events (deaths, divorce, violence), children may believe they are experiencing a crisis even if they don't know what to call it.

Today's young people are regularly confronted with events which they see as crises. The degree of success they demonstrate in coping with such crises varies widely. The trial-and-error methods of coping with crises employed by many young people have been less than effective because these young people often fail to utilize the support systems available to them.

A common technique with which young people attempt to deal with crises is denial. This offers some short term relief from stress, but does not provide a method facing issues any more effectively in the future. School systems which do not acknowledge the crises of their students are also practicing denial. To understand the long range implications for both students and school systems, we must ask: What are the effects of stress? and What effect, if any, will this have on student behavior?

EFFECTS ON STUDENTS OF CRISES AND LOSS

Crises have associated losses, whether actual or threatened. These include: loss of friends or loved ones, relationships, security, hope, health, feelings of trust, or even the loss of childhood innocence. This forcible loss of something or someone precious is known as *bereavement*. When dealing with bereavement, children may react in any of a variety of ways. Both children and their schools must learn to cope with behaviors which may include:

- emotional numbing—This can vary from a brief period of shock, to a reaction where children believe, in effect, that if feelings hurt this much, they refuse to feel anything at all.
- guilt/anger—these two feelings are often linked and may result in apathy (a withdrawing from life) or in acting out. This acting out from guilt and/or anger may be directed at others through verbal or even physical attacks. It can also be directed back at the child him/herself in a pattern of "accidents" or punishment seeking behavior.
- fear of the future—The future is unknown and children may fear they will be unable to cope with crises that could arise in this unknown future. Examples of this fear may be seen in students who resist any further changes in their lives or their environment. This can be taken to a point where a student may even deliberately fail to avoid the changes, and losses, which would accompany graduation. These fears, if unaddressed, may even develop into a type of free-floating anxiety where every change requiring action on the part of the individual becomes an immediate crisis.

The effects of anxiety on schoolwork have been demonstrated by a number of researchers, including Gaudry and Speilberger [1] and Behrens, et al. [2]. Students experience a shorter attention span and difficulty in concentrating which is often accompanied by a drop in grades. In varying degrees, many of these students perceive themselves to be "helpless" in coping with crises and have shown signs of depression, increased episodes of daydreaming, and withdrawal from socialization with peers. These students also report somatic complaints more often than their peers.

Returning to our earlier definitions of crises, we can now ask: Are there some crises which occur in the lives of our children with enough frequency that all schools should have a plan to assist students facing these crises?

PREPARING STUDENTS

It is now widely held that the most effective way of assisting people to cope more effectively with crises is to do so in advance of the actual event or situation. After the onset of a crisis there can be a period of "psychic annulment." This concept was first used by Caprio in 1950 to describe the difficulty people have assimilating information in times of crisis [3]. He applied the concept to grief following a death, but it has wide applicability to individuals in crises. To state that an attempt to develop and implement effective support systems for students or protocols for dealing with a crisis in the midst of the crisis is not effective is a gross understatement. In times of crisis, there is not the luxury of having *time* . . . time for reflection, time for evaluation, time for education of staff and parents or time for implementation in a calm and thoughtful manner.

Programs now exist or are in the process of development for helping students, educators and parents to cope with some growing crises. These programs address grief and loss, youth suicide, health issues (including both life threatening illness and sexually transmitted diseases), violence in our society (including assault, rape, and violent death), and war (with its special impact on the military family).

Can school programs prevent or lessen the pain of loss, or prevent trauma in times of crisis? The answer is probably *no*. No program can prevent the pain of loss or the traumatic impact of a crisis. However, if students and staff are prepared for possible crises, such preparation may keep the traumatic effects from being worse than they may otherwise have to be. In times of crisis and their aftermath, people feel a loss of control over their lives. This is especially true in the case of children and adolescents who may already be dealing with feelings of helplessness from prior losses and/or who may feel powerless in a world run by adults. Programs which have been shown to help young people in crisis have some points in common. These programs:

- help students by increasing feelings of self-worth and existing programs can be a resource in times of crisis,
- show students how they can draw on support systems, such as family, friends, educators, and/or religious advisors,
- help students to develop a belief that they have an internal center of control over events in their lives,
- allow students to feel more secure in a hostile world,
- assist students to identify and cope with feelings of guilt which may accompany a significant loss,
- explain the process of grief, which helps people to recover from bereavement,
- explain that even when everything is done in the "right way" crises can still occur and that a crisis (whether it be due to a death, or a change in family structure, or illness) is not necessarily anyone's "fault."

Life is filled with changes for a child and each change carries with it potential losses. After a loss occurs, it grows far more difficult to provide effective interventions. In order to help children prepare to live through the losses they will inevitably encounter, we must take action before the loss occurs, not after the fact.

WHEN GRIEF IS A CRISIS

Death touches the lives of all of us. Children are by no means immune. By senior year in high school, one in twenty children will have had a parent die. Each year one in every 750 school-age children dies. To these personal tragedies, we can add the deaths of other relatives, the deaths of school staff members, the deaths of family pets (which are both personal and meaningful deaths to many adults as well as children), and the death experience encountered by families dealing with stillbirth or miscarriage. Children who are coping with such losses will need to find a way to cope with their grief.

The grief process is, in most cases, a healing process. However, it is not one that occurs without sadness or apart from the emotional pain associated with loss. It is also not a process where the individual can remain passive and simply "wait" for things to get better. It requires a bereaved individual to complete certain "tasks." These tasks facing bereaved children were defined by Sandra Fox. [4] The four tasks she enumerated served as the basis for her "Good Grief Program" in Boston, Massachusetts. She believed that to successfully complete the grief process, a child needs to:

1. *UNDERSTAND* — The child must understand that *death is universal*. All things that live will, one day, die. It is no one's "fault" that things are this way. This is simply part of life. The child must understand that the deceased person no longer feels anything because a dead body no longer functions as it once did. Finally, the child, apart from the religious beliefs of his/her family, must understand that the physical aspects of death are irreversible. *Death is permanent*.
2. *GRIEVE* — There are many feelings connected with bereavement, especially sadness, anger and guilt. The child must be able to both *experience and to express the feelings that are part of the grief process*.
3. *COMMEMORATE* — The child needs to remember the life of the person who died, both good things and bad, to *mourn the real person* who is gone. Where possible, the child should also play some role in helping to decide how the deceased will be remembered.
4. *MOVE ON* — When the child has moved through the grief process, he/she will need to take the final step of getting on with

life. It is necessary to return to the business of being a child with all of the living, loving and learning that childhood entails.

An individual death or an injury to a friend or family member may, at first, present a crisis to a single child. However, this crisis extends to other members of the school community when this child returns to interact with teachers and classmates or when, as often happens, it is someone in the school community who is asked to inform the child.

As with other crises, thoughtful preparation can help educators to avoid some common pitfalls when faced with the difficult task of informing a student of the death or injury of a loved one. Educators should work together to develop guidelines that meet their needs and reflect the needs, values and traditions of the community as a whole. Questions to be answered by such guidelines include:

Who should inform the student? The student should be told by someone he/she sees as an authority figure. An administrator typically assumes this role. Someone who has a close relationship with the student (teacher, nurse, counselor, or fellow student) should be with the student and should be able to remain after the student receives the news.

Where should the student be told? The student should be taken to a place where he/she can have *privacy*. The student should be able to sit or to lie down if necessary. In most schools, these requirements are met by the school nurse's office.

How should the student be told? The student should be told what has happened in a quiet, simple and direct manner. Platitudes or religious symbolism should be avoided. These may have great meaning to the adult but may be confusing or upsetting to the child. The child's questions should be answered openly and honestly but unnecessary details need not be volunteered. Emotions and feelings should not be avoided (and, yes, big boys *do* cry and should be allowed to if they feel the need). This time can allow the student to begin to sort out confusing feelings and can help him/her to see the school in a supportive role, even at a later date. In all of this, the wishes of the family, if they are known, should be respected as much as possible.

How will a student react? After a student has received the news, he or she may have any of a number of possible reactions. Educators must remember that there is no one "correct" response. Physical contact, such as touching a shoulder or holding a hand, may have a calming effect, but not all students feel comfortable with this. If a student merely wishes to sit, this wish should be respected. However, the student should not be left alone. If the student remains silent, inform him/her that it is all right to speak about feelings.

It is essential that staff reaction to a student not appear judgmental. It would be unwise, for example, to minimize an event such as the death of a pet. In the overall functioning of the school, the death of a pet may not seem to an administrator to be a crisis. However, the young person involved may have just learned of the death of a lifelong friend who provided companionship and love. Or, a student's reaction to *this* news may be difficult to understand until we remember that it does not occur in a vacuum and other prior events may be the reason for the reaction we now see.

Who else should be informed? The family should be aware of what the student was told and all of the child's teachers, the school nurse, and school counselors should be informed of the situation as soon as possible.

A protocol to address the needs of an individual student is not directly transferrable when it is the entire school community that is affected. If for no other reason, the number of students affected make it virtually impossible to cope with the situation on an individual basis. Such a crisis required the cooperation of all school personnel. Coordinating such an effort requires further advance planning. The questions to be answered are similar, but the answers may differ.

Where should the students be told? It is "efficient" to bring all students together in an auditorium to inform them of some crisis. However, such large group disclosures lack any shred of privacy, block the release of emotions, and hinder identification of students who may need special attention. For these reasons large group presentations are almost always less beneficial for individual students. Whenever possible, students should receive the news of a crisis situation in familiar surroundings with people they know and trust. The classroom offers such a setting.

How should the students be told? Preselected staff members will be sent to inform all students of the event(s) that has occurred. Not every educator will be comfortable performing such a task and this must be determined in advance. The team of educators (called a "crisis response team" in some districts) should receive additional training concerning student needs in times of grief and/or stress. The same information should be given to all students. The information should be given in a calm, direct manner and the team members should stay to assist the classroom teacher in answering questions and addressing feelings and reactions. The school nurse is sometimes assigned the role of informing students. However, experience has shown that some students may experience physical distress or have specific somatic complaints and will need the nurse to be available to perform her primary task as a medical professional. The nurse is too valuable in that role to be assigned a task that would make her unavailable to a large segment of the student body.

How will the students react? While it is difficult to predict the reaction of an individual student, the reaction of groups of students is somewhat predictable. Some students will feel sad or angry and will express these feelings. Other students may feel guilty and seek to withdraw from interaction with peers or teachers. A third group of students will not appear to feel anything at all. Some students may actually not be affected by the news or feel any personal involvement. However, there are students who *appear* uninvolved but are actually seeking to mask thoughts or feelings with which they are uncomfortable. There are others who actually do not "feel" any reaction and are scared that they do not. It is essential that students be helped to understand that virtually all of these reactions are "normal" because, however the individual student reacts, it is a response shared with many others. What may cause concern is the intensity of individual reactions. Any school protocol must provide assistance for those students who need individual assistance. Again, there are people already in the schools who have this task as part of their job descriptions. School counselors, however, are forced to be so involved with college selection and mandated testing programs that their skills as counselors have at times not kept pace with current practice. To maintain and enhance staff skills in this area, training and workshops should be provided for counselors, social workers, school nurses and interested teachers on a regular basis.

Who else should be informed? All staff members must be kept informed of the details of events related to this crisis. Parents must be kept informed of the actions taken in school and of the events which affect their children. Other community leaders (religious leaders, health professionals, uniformed services, and political leaders) should also be part of the information network. All communication must be two-way. School officials and teachers must solicit and be responsive to input from parents and the community as a whole. In times of crisis, no section of the community should be denied a chance to assist affected young people.

What issues can complicate student reaction and/or school response? Certain events have been found to be factors which may produce complicated student reactions in times of crisis. The type of death can produce a grief reaction which is different from that which follows a death caused by illness or accident. Grief after a suicide is such an type of death. Those who are alive after someone they loved, knew or identified with dies as the result of a completed suicide are called *survivors of suicide*. The grief of these survivors is different for one or more of the following reasons:

- It is sudden and seldom anticipated.
- It is often violent.
- It takes place in the presence of other stressors.
- It accentuates feelings of "regret" and/or "guilt."
- Survivors experience a feeling of loss of control over the events in their lives.
- Loss of control is made worse by a flood of emotions.
- Society's reaction is often negative or judgmental.
- Survivors feel they are being "avoided" by others. [5, p. 13]

A death from AIDS can also complicate the grief reaction and create a situation in which young people may have special needs. AIDS-related grief can produce:

- isolation — friends of family members of the deceased being avoided through fear or misunderstanding;
- lack of social support — memorials or other rituals which typically follow a death are sometimes not available after an AIDS related death;
- feelings of guilt — social sanctions may cause special feelings of guilt for those students who were friends of the deceased, or who believe they have engaged in "high-risk" behavior;
- anger/violence — Strong emotions may be released within the school community and if there is no outlet provided, these feelings can produce incidents of violence. [6]

Crises do not only occur after a death. *Violence* in the schools is growing at a rapid rate. It might comfort some to think that this is a phenomenon linked only to inner-city schools but violence is reaching into every area of the country with greater frequency. It may be the random violence of a drive-by "gang-banging" or the more selective violence of an act of self-destruction. When violent attack takes place or a death has occurred as the result of violence the pain and confusion left in its wake can touch every student in a school, or in many schools. However, the *possibility* of violence is a crisis which is faced by students and by schools across the country on a daily basis. Some schools have reacted to an episode of violence by starting programs to address students' feelings of a lack of security and their need to address issues involving personal safety. However, now is the time for all schools to become proactive by addressing these needs among their students and a possible side-effect may well be the prevention of the violence itself.

A similar conclusion can be drawn about health issues connected to HIV and AIDS. A school can deny the real risk confronting students who may be sexually active or be engaged in other behaviors, such as drug abuse. They can say there is no crisis because no deaths have occurred or because no students are yet *known* to be HIV positive. However, television, radio, movies, and newspapers are filled with stories on a daily basis that show the immunity which students feel, and schools seemingly reinforce with their silence, is only an illusion. Although it may not be as openly acknowledged as the concern over violence, the *possibility* of contracting an HIV infection or of AIDS is one that exists in every school in this country. We can again try to distance ourselves with myths. Just as we might want to believe that violence "only" takes place in urban schools, we may try to draw comfort from the belief in the myth that AIDS is a "gay disease." By focusing on, and isolating, one element of the school community, this illusion can reduce anxiety for many in the short term, but in the long run it may prove fatal for some and can be harmful for everyone. The continuation of student behaviors which place them at risk, whether from violence or from HIV/AIDS, is a crisis which must be addressed by the whole community. If parents and educators work together now to help our children, it can avoid the finger-pointing and accusations later, when it may too late for some young people and the crises faced by the survivors will have multiplied.

STRESS AND CRISES

Crises do not necessarily occur only during, or in the wake of, a particular event. The lives of young people are filled with "pressures." These pressures can cause some of these young people to believe that they have less and less control over their own lives. Increasingly our young people show an inability to deal with loss, both present and possible future losses. They attempt to avoid reality through elaborate patterns of denial which may even include high-risk, "death defying" behavior. They demonstrate increasing inability to adjust to change at the same time that their lives are filled with an ever-growing number of physical, emotional, environmental and physical changes. Their bodies are changing. They are moving into and out of new relationships. They may find themselves uprooted and dropped into new circumstances as a result of the demands that society makes on their parents. Young people must attempt to deal with parental absence caused by divorce or death, and with the conflict that often appears between the ideal family they learn about or wish for and the real one in which they live. Finally, our young people suffer from an ability to meet goals set by themselves or others for their lives and future. This sense of "failure," whether real or imaginary, causes suffering that, if left unaddressed has prompted attempts at "self-medication" with alcohol or drugs and increasingly in a growing number of self-destructive acts by our young people.

A school may develop a protocol to assist young people to deal with a crisis, but what if the crisis is multiple? What if there are many crises to be addressed by a student or students and not only the issue which is most current? Faced with *multiple* crises, the real crisis faced by young people may well be a belief that they have lost control over their lives. They would like to try to regain control but, faced with so many crises, they simply don't know where to begin. This personal sense of crisis is real for so many students that it too becomes an issue to be addressed by the caring adults in their lives.

ADDRESSING MULTIPLE CRISES

A protocol for educators and/or parents who seek to assist adolescents in coping with multiple crises should consider the following points. They are based, in part, on the observations of high school students who have encountered just the sort of multiple crises that such a protocol seeks to address. These students believe that adults who wish to help must learn to:

- *LISTEN* — Are you listening to what these young people are actually saying, or are you thinking of possible future answers or actions while they are still telling their stories?
- *IDENTIFY AND LIST CRISES (both past and present)* — A long list may appear frightening, but it could become a source of strength. After all, it shows the young person just how many crises they have been able to cope with in the past. It can also explain to a distressed individual how past crises have combined to make this "latest" crisis may have been so upsetting.
- *ESTABLISH PRIORITIES* — Ask, "What do *you* want to deal with first?" This is a starting point in having the young person identify the meaning that he/she has attributed to each event. Each crisis or loss may be viewed differently, even by the same individual. How does the young person view each crisis with its attendant losses? Has it created a *void,* an empty part of a life that needs to be filled? Is it an *enemy,* which needs to be overcome? Is it a *gain,* which may afford attention or a period of release from "pressure?"

Is this crisis *actual* (in the past or present) or *anticipated* (a possible future event)? Identifying the nature of the crisis can, at times, show the young person possible courses of action to address the situation.

- *HELP THE YOUNG PERSON TO FOCUS ON ONE CRISIS AT A TIME* — Avoid the overwhelming situation of trying to deal with all things at once or the confusion of moving too quickly from one issue to another.
- *REMIND THE YOUNG PERSON THAT EACH OF US HAS BOTH A RIGHT AND A RESPONSIBILITY TO LET OTHERS KNOW OF OUR LOSSES IF WE EXPECT THEM TO ACT TOWARD US IN AN "APPROPRIATE" WAY IN TIMES OF CRISIS* — If a loss has made a person different in some way and others are unaware of the loss, it may not be possible for them to act toward that person in an appropriate way. If the person needs support, he/she has a responsibility to let others know of the loss. If that person needs to speak of the loss, he/she has a right to do so.
- *REMEMBER THAT THE SCHOOL'S FUNCTION IS TO EDUCATE THE "WHOLE PERSON"* — It is not a disembodied intellect that comes into the school. These young people bring past histories and personal issues which have a major effect on the learning process. It cannot and should not be the primary function of educators to assist young people with "life crises." Educating students as they seek to learn the volume of academic content in a typical school curriculum is the school's primary task. Despite the many changes taking place in today's world, parents are still the first teachers of their children and are a key factor in determining the stability, values and mores in a child's life. However, there are many areas in which educators and parents can work together for the benefit of the children about whom they both care.

SCHOOL-BASED "THERAPIES"

It is important to remember that while activities in a classroom may produce therapeutic benefits for some students, the only thing which can be "cured" in a class setting is ignorance. Education is what is provided by teachers and schools and there is no need to apologize for an increase of knowledge on the part of students. However, therapy is best left to mental health professionals (guidance counselors, social workers, school psychologists, doctors, and nurses). Decisions about the lives of young people are ultimately the responsibility of those young people and their parents. However, nothing is so easily compartmentalized in the real world. All of the caring adults in the life of a young person can make contributions to the education, emotional health and future well-being of the young people in their care.

The age of the child is always a factor. Some well-intentioned people have attempted to take programs developed for adolescents and use them with much younger students. This may be a mistake and can be harmful. The best way to avoid such a mistake while trying to help a child is through open communication among all parties about the needs and welfare of the child involved. Parents/guardians must be involved in the lives of their children and, in most cases, it is wrong for the school to exclude them. Parents too should be willing to draw on the educators in their children's lives and to make them part of a support system for their children. This sort of communication has been shown to have a positive effect on academic performance and can have a similar benefit for the child's emotional well being. When such communication does not take place on a regular basis and there is a separation between home and school, it does not benefit the children.

CONCLUSION

Prior planning is the most effective way for schools to prepare students and staff to deal with the crises we may encounter in life. However, it is not possible to develop protocols for every possible crises which could possibly occur. Even if there were time enough to do so (which there is not), or space in an already crowded school day (which may be made available but is limited), who would possibly be able to predict what the future may hold? What then are educators to do? What should parents expect from their children's schools? To help students cope with crises, parents and educators can encourage schools to take the following steps:

- develop and implement educational programs for teachers, students and parents dealing with those crises which currently exist, such as adolescent suicide prevention, HIV/AIDS, and/or violence.
- develop protocols for use when crises occur which identify in advance key individuals, resources, and support groups. Part of this should involve a process for creating and implementing new protocols and for reevaluating and/or revising older ones when necessary.
- create a task force of educators, parents, and community members to be the focal point of intervention efforts when crises do occur.

- develop and *maintain* an ongoing program of staff development, with parent and community outreach components, to prepare all members of the academic community to be potential resources in times of crisis.
- open and maintain lines of communication among all parties, teachers, counselors, parents, and students which can be used to convey good news as well as bad and can combat the potential harm caused by rumor or ignorance of important information.

REFERENCES

1. E. Gaudry, and C. Speilberger, *Anxiety and Educational Achievement,* J. Wiley and Sons Australasia, Sydney, Australia, 1971.
2. R. Behrens, et al. A Descriptive Study of Elementary School Children Who Have Suffered A Major Loss, Master's Thesis, Simmons College of Social Work, 1964, cited by H. Moller in *Explaining Death to Children,* E. A. Grollman (ed.), Beacon Press, Boston, Massachusetts, p. 164, 1967.
3. F. S. Caprio, A Study of Some Psychological Reactions During Prepubescence to the Idea of Death, *Psychiatric Quarterly, 24,* p. 495, 1950.
4. S. S. Fox, Good Grief: Positive Interventions for Children and Adolescents, *Preventive Psychiatry: Early Intervention and Situational Crisis Management,* S. C. Klagsbrun, et al. (eds.), Charles Press, Philadelphia, pp. 83-92, 1989.
5. E. J. Dunne, J. L. McIntosh, and K. Dunne-Maxim (eds.), *Suicide and Its Aftermath: Understanding and Counseling the Survivors,* W.W. Norton and Company, New York, 1987.
6. R. G. Stevenson, AIDS Related Grief: Helping Young People to Understand the Impact of Societal Values on the Grief Process, Illness, *Crises and Loss, 1*:2, pp. 56-59, 1991.

BIBLIOGRAPHY

Grollman, E. A., *Talking About Death: A Dialogue Between Parent and Child,* Beacon Press, Boston, Massachusetts, 1990.

Stevenson, R. G., The Child and Suffering: The Role of the School, in *Suffering: Psychological and Social Aspects in Loss, Grief and Care,* R. DeBellis, et al. (eds.), Haworth Press, New York, pp. 151-153, 1986.

Stevenson, R. G., Death Education as a Preventive Approach in Promoting Mental Health, in *Preventive Psychiatry: Early Intervention and Situation Crisis Management*, S. C. Klagsbrun et al. (eds.), Charles Press, Philadelphia, p. 155-160, 1989.

Stevenson, R. G., Students, Stress and Burnout, in *Professional Burnout In Medicine and the Helping Professions,* D. T. Wessells, Jr., et al. (eds.), Haworth Press, New York, p. 33-38, 1989.

Stevenson, R. G. and J. O. Brett, Dealing With the Impact of 'Community' Grief, in *Bereavement: Helping the Survivors*, M. A. Morgan (ed.), King's College, London, Ontario, pp. 275-282, 1987.

Stevenson, R. G. and H. Powers, How To Handle Death in the School, *Tips For Principals,* December 1986.

Stevenson, R. G., Teen Suicide: Sources, Signals and Prevention, in *The Dying and Bereaved Teenager,* J. D. Morgan, (ed.), Charles Press, Philadelphia, pp. 135-139, 1990.

CHAPTER 2

Preparing Schools for Crisis Management

Margaret Metzgar

How many teachers, at Hubbard Woods Elementary School, do you think went to school on that morning in May expecting that by the end of the day one of their students would be shot to death and four others injured? Do you really think that the kindergarten teachers that took their students to see the world trade center ever expected to be trapped on top, victims of a terrorist bomb? Would you have been prepared to handle the devastation, in Homestead Florida, following hurricane Andrew's rage? How do you deal with the educational needs of students when there isn't even a school left standing? How would your school respond to a third grader being shot, in class, by one of her classmates? How prepared do you feel to stand, looking into the innocent faces of a sixth grade class, and explain that their friend killed himself last night?

These are not isolated situations. Pick up any newspaper, on any day anywhere in the nation, and you will find examples of schools forced to deal with some form of a crises. In 1990, 45,169 children between the ages of five and twenty-four died across the United States [1]. That equals approximately 124 child deaths a day, or six children dying each hour of the day, twenty-four hours a day. According to the 1991 Uniform Crime Report 3,787 children under the age of eighteen died as a result of homicide (2,702 between the ages of 15 to 19). Out of those, where the age of both the victim and offender could be determined, in 295 cases both victim and offender were under the age of nineteen. Morley Shafer, on *60 Minutes,* recently reported that, "By one estimate, 90,000 children in this country now carry guns to school" [2].

Seldom are we given advanced warning of a specific upcoming crisis so we can prepare a response. It is also true, unfortunately, that many schools still subscribe to the "it will never happen here" philosophy. Then, when the crisis does happen, they find themselves in a very uncomfortable, unprepared, reactive rather than proactive position.

The keys to successful crisis management are preplanning and preparation. These need to begin long before there is even a hint of a crisis and must extend beyond the internal workings of the district or school. Good preplanning demands the creation and ongoing development of a strong *internal school support structure*, an *external community support structure*, and a *communication network* that enables both to respond on a moments notice. The internal structure includes administrators, teachers, students and parents. The external structure expands those resources to include; crisis trained emergency services personnel (police and fire), mental health professionals, religious and community leaders, as well as, local businesses, hospitals, and media.

Granted, many minor school crises can and will be handled internally. However, the situation at Hubbard Wood Elementary is a good example of how the internal structure and external community support can work together for a successful outcome. Within minutes of Laurie Dann entering this school and shooting five children, police and emergency medical personnel were on the scene. The injured children were taken to the hospital and the other children were kept in their classrooms, where it was believed to be safe. Their telephone tree was immediately put into action. The calls had two purposes: to reassure parents and gain their help. Within thirty minutes, the psychologist, social workers from the hospital, as well as, private practitioners, clergy and parents had arrived to offer assistance. Because no one knew where Laurie Dann had gone it was decided that the safest place for the children was in the school. The local McDonalds sent Chicken McNuggets and fries for lunch. The superintendent of schools and chief of police spoke to the parents while the principal went to each classroom to tell the kids exactly what had happened. Before the parents took their children home they had been told what to expect by a mental health professional. This all took place on Friday. On Saturday the parents were asked to return with their children to the school in order to meet again with the school principal and community mental health specialists. This was just the first of many family meetings organized by the school with the assistance of those mental health specialists. By all reports this community has been drawn even closer together, in the aftermath of this crisis, thanks to the successful joint school and community efforts. We could all take a lesson from this situation.

Using that example as a back drop will help those caring adults who wish to look at crisis preparedness in their schools. The information in this chapter is designed to help any school create or review their current crisis management plan, with emphasis on community involvement. Given the proper preparation and implementation of a crisis plan, schools that encounter crises situations can experience this type of successful outcome. For over seven years I have been teaching a class called *Crisis! Not My School!!* This is a class for educators, administrators and entire school communities. The course is an attempt to assist these caring adults to explore their crisis response needs and review their existing plans. The material contained in this chapter is information that was gathered or created for that class. It is presented here in an abridged version but it uses the same step by step sequential, systematic process I use in that class [3].

CRISIS PLANNING AND PREPARATION

Formation of a Steering Committee

Planning and preparation begin first with the formation of a steering committee. It will be their task to systematically explore all the schools' needs related to crisis management. The steering committee is sometimes confused with the crisis response team. It is possible, even recommended, that the membership of these two committees overlap. However, it is important to keep in mind the distinct differences in the two committees. The "steering committee" has the *proactive responsibility* (preparation and prevention). This responsibility includes tasks such as: defining what is a crisis, creating a crisis plan, and training all staff to implement the plan. The "crisis response team" has the *reactive responsibility* (intervention and postvention). The team responds during or following the crisis by putting the crisis response plan, designed by the steering committee, into action. Since, the focus of this chapter is on preparing schools for crisis management, we will examine the proactive tasks of the steering committee in detail. Other chapters will address the reactive tasks of crisis response.

Membership of the steering committee should not be limited to school personnel. Ideally, this committee will be composed of four to six committed, high-energy people who are willing to accept the responsibility of exploring all aspects of crisis management as it relates to their individual school. This is a working committee. Diversity and community support are a must. Members can include:

- one or two concerned teachers,
- a counselor or school psychologist,
- the principal or designate,
- at least one community resource person (i.e., a representative from the emergency medical services, a local mental health professional, or a spiritual or religious advisor), and
- a parent or PTSA/PTO member.

Remember schools do not exist in a vacuum. Most crises that occur within a school have potential reverberations throughout the school community. Involving the community, from the beginning, will help built the cohesiveness that was shown by the previous example.

Defining a Crisis and Determining the Level of Response

The twin responsibilities of defining a crisis and determining the level of response are the first tasks of the steering committee. On the surface that may seem silly. We like to believe that everybody knows what a crisis is. But let's take a moment and explore the traditional definition of crisis to see if it fits the school setting. A crisis is most often thought of as an unexpected event that requires an emergency or immediate response. That definition certainly fits the opening examples and would be applicable to a gang shooting, a fire in the school, a child abduction or a whole list of other unexpected events. However, based on that definition, is the death of a student during summer vacation a *crisis*? How can there be an immediate response? Does the expected death of a child or teacher, to cancer for example, fit that crisis definition? It seems that such an event, clearly one with huge implications for any school system, requires a different definition. My experience has led me to define a school crisis as any situation that causes, or has the potential to cause, a disruption of normal functioning within the school community. This includes any situation with potential risk to the physical or emotional safety and well being of the students.

Crises come in all shapes and sizes. They vary in degree of severity as well as the level, or extent, of intervention required. Some originate within the school. Others originate outside the school, yet have direct impact on the school. It is recommended that a school plan make the distinction between an *internal* and *external* crisis. The rationale for making distinctions between types of crisis is that such a distinction helps to decide such issues as:

- who is in charge,
- the amount of school, district or extended community support required,
- the amount of media or press involvement, etc.

Internal Crises

An internal crisis is one which occurs within the school community. Its impact can either be limited to the school or it can have effects that reach far beyond the school boundaries.

External Crises

An external crisis is one which occurs outside the school, be it in the community, nation or world. Yet, the impact reverberates throughout the school and must be dealt with by the school.

Levels of Crises

Some schools also like to define levels of crisis. Those definitions are usually based directly upon the number of students, or members of the school community directly affected and level of intervention required. It is the steering committee's responsibility to create a crisis management plan flexible enough to address the full range of potential crises.

All school crises, internal or external, have the potential for impacting the physical and emotional safety and security of students, as well as their educational performance. The extent of the impact is directly dependent upon the severity of trauma/crisis and how well the crisis is handled. Though the actual crisis may be short in duration and may have limited physical safety implications, the emotional or educational effects may be life long. Any number of studies have shown that emotional trauma resulting from a crisis may have long term emotional impact. In addition, a crisis may profoundly effect a students' ability to concentrate, thereby potentially impacting their educational performance and educational future.

Defining Goals

Defining goals for successful crisis management is the next task for the steering committee. These goals need to reflect the physical, emotional and educational needs, of the school community during and after a crisis. The following three goals offer a sample of crisis response goals that you might consider.

During a school crisis all school personnel must:

1. Provide first and always for the physical safety of all school community members;
2. Minimize the emotional trauma resulting from the impact of the crisis;
3. Manage the crisis so that it becomes a learning opportunity, contributing to the overall educational goals of promoting students' growth [3, 27].

Allowing these three goals to direct your actions will be helpful in putting together responses for specific types or levels of crisis. Even though there is no substitute for the nuclear family, today's schools are being call on, more than ever before, to respond to the emotional and physical needs, as well as the educational needs of their students. This is especially true in times of crisis. Hopefully, having parent and community representatives on the steering committee will help to encourage parent/family involvement and support during a crisis.

Successful execution of a crisis management plan is primarily dependent upon the preplanning of the steering committee. It is their responsibility to ask and answer crisis questions in advance, and to insure that everyone is prepared. This may mean confronting school and community denial in order to persuade members of the whole school community that a crisis will touch their lives. One of the potential stumbling blocks for a steering committee is resistance.

Resistance refers to efforts by members of some people (acting as individuals or groups) to block the work of the steering committee, or to a determined, continual lack of cooperation with such work. Resistance is very common when addressing such topics as death, grief, loss, or crisis in relationship to children. These topics tap into many personal fears, denial or a desire to "protect" the children. In addition, they bring moral, religious and spiritual beliefs into question. Failure to address resistance is frequently a cause for difficulty in crisis management. If their resistance is not addressed, these individuals may later undo the planning of the steering committee, even during a crisis.

It will be up to the committee to evaluate the level of resistance within their school. Are there potential sources of resistance that need to be addressed? Are there teachers who don't want to talk about death because they don't know what to say or are afraid they might "fall apart?" Is there a principal that is afraid that if you talk about Johnny's suicide you will "give other students ideas?" Are there community members that are offended if you want to talk about AIDS or death? Has there been such resistance to parts of other school programs, such as sex education or family living?

Can the resistance that exists within each school community be identified? Are there key individuals (counselors, ministers) or groups who might be helpful in addressing these resistances? Resistance must be identified and addressed directly in order to develop school and community ownership of any plan.

Creating a Community Profile

Crisis plans need to reflect a community profile. This includes the demographics of the community and the statistical prediction as to type of crisis most likely to be experienced in that area. Schools, communities and geography vary widely. That is why it is impossible to create a universal crisis management plan. Individualization of a crisis response plan is recommended. That individualization will be dependent upon the many complex characteristics present in a school and in its surrounding community. Reviewing these characteristics is important so that the plan that is developed is designed with this school's specific needs in mind. For instance it would be silly for a Fargo, North Dakota school to have an "ash fall" plan. However, that proved to be an important plan for Washington schools located near Mt. St. Helen's.

Community profile characteristics might include:

- geography,
- cultural and ethnic diversity,
- political and social factors,
- religious and philosophical beliefs,
- local language/dialects,
- socio-economic status, and
- other specific unique community characteristics; and resources available.

This list is not meant to be exhaustive, but to increase sensitivity to some of the many possible factors influencing crisis response. To aid in the development of a community profile let's take a brief look at each of those characteristics individually and how they may apply.

Geography

As was the case near Mount St. Helen, geography can play a very important part in the types of crises you may experience. It is also something over which we have little control. The geographic region will not always be an indicator of the kind of natural disaster for which a school needs to be prepared, but it may give some vital clues. Is this region more likely to experience an earthquake, flood, tornado, hurricane, volcanic eruption, excessive snow fall or some other type of natural disaster? Are all necessary personnel prepared for these types of natural disasters?

Cultural and Ethnic Diversity

Both are common in schools today. As much as that diversity is welcome, it also creates its own implications for crisis response. It is important to consider the values of various ethnic and cultural groups in determining the school's response to a crisis. Recognition of ethnic rituals and cultural norms related to violence, death and loss should be included as part of the response to a crisis. It is also important to be in direct communication with leaders of ethnic communities if the crisis involves an ethnic or racial incident. In fact, if there is a large ethnic population in a school, it may be advisable to invite one or more leaders of that group to be a part of the steering committee.

Political and Social Factors

The political and social "climate" of the school and community may also be important considerations in developing a crisis response plan. These factors, much like ethnic and culture diversity, can influence social traditions or mores, including attitudes toward crises and loss. A highly conservative community, for example, may have very strong feelings about the role they want the school to play in discussing death or unwanted pregnancy. This is just one of many possible examples but it underscores the importance of having key leaders, representing all elements of a community, involved.

Religious and Philosophical Implications

The topic of crisis, especially one involving a death, is also heavy laden with religious and philosophical implications. Individual/family beliefs are often strong and may be powerful determinants of students' interpretations of a crisis and its effects. These beliefs must be respected and need to be handled with sensitivity when dealing with a crisis, especially in a public school setting. For example. it has been found that when a crisis involves the death of a student, it may be helpful to have a leader of that student's religious group consult with the crisis response team.

Language Following a Crisis

Many schools struggle with language following a crisis. If your school has a bilingual or multilingual population it is especially important to provide skilled interpreters during times of crisis. When under stress, children and adults typically revert back to their primary language. What languages are represented in your school? It is also important to remember that, whenever possible, written and verbal communication from the school to parents or community members should be available in the primary language spoken by a student and/or family.

Socio-Economic Status

Socio-economic status also plays a role. The financial resources available within families effect what services the school must provide, and what follow-up assistance may be available outside the school. For example, in an affluent community, the crisis plan may direct school personnel to provide lists of community mental health agencies to families who wish to pursue this option. However, where people lack the resources to pursue private counseling, the school may need to bring professionals to the school to meet with students and families.

Unique Community Characteristics

In addition to those factors already mentioned, a steering committee must ask what other specific unique characteristics may be present in this community or school. Examples might include:

- a school located on or near a military base,
- a school located in the inner city,
- a school located in a farm community with numbers of migrant laborers, or
- a school with students who don't have homes but instead live in a shelter for the homeless or on the streets.

Whatever the unique community features might be, the steering committee should ask itself whether there are any unique factors in their community that should be considered when developing the crisis management plan.

Community Resources

A final, yet critical, consideration involves the identification of outside resources. What community emergency services are available (e.g., police, fire department, emergency medical services, even the F.B.I.)? How can they be contacted? What are the important phone numbers? What professional mental health services (especially psychologists or counselors who specialize in issues of grief and loss and/or crisis response) can be available? Are there national organizations (such as MADD or SADD) that may provide helpful contacts in the aftermath of a crisis? Which community or religious organizations will be asked for help? All of these resources should be contacted and interviewed *in advance*. Don't forget the importance of parental support and involvement, get the PTSA/PTO active in your efforts. Their members may have outside resources or contacts upon which the school can draw.

Financial Factors

When looking at resources, money is always a factor. Many organizations will offer help free of charge, or for a nominal charge, in times of crisis. However, there may be items that require funds. The steering committee may choose to address this issue and determine what funds are available in an emergency and who it is that will be authorized to expend those funds?

The bulk of the community profile will never appear on the actual crisis plan. It should be viewed as a thought problem or a worksheet. Its purpose is to promote thoughts that will help individualize a crisis management plan.

Concrete Tasks of Crisis Management

Once the foundation is laid, you have defined crisis, reviewed your goals, examined possible sources of resistance, and developed your community profile, you are ready to begin dealing with the concrete tasks of crisis management.

1. *Determine whether there are any existing district or building plans.* Most schools have some form of a disaster plan, some are extensive, while some are found only in the heads of an administrator. Next, look at what the plan covers. It is frequently the case that district and/or school plans are limited to reactive plans that have been created in the wake of a crisis. Many school plans are limited to fire or natural disaster responses and do not address dealing with sudden trauma, the death of a student, teacher, or family member, gang violence, etc. Does your school plan deal with internal *personal* crises as well as fire, natural disasters or external crises?

As the steering committee gathers together all plans currently in use, there are additional questions to be answered. Are the plans up to date? When were they last reviewed? Who knows about the plans? Are they available in writing? Sadly, many school plans are not written and/or distributed among the staff. *Poor communication can defeat even the best laid plans.* Are your plans referenced in the teachers' handbook? . . . in the parents' handbook? . . . in the students' handbook?

When was the last time there was a crisis management plan discussed during in-service training? Have key personnel ever had a crisis drill (for other than a fire)? Should a crisis occur is the plan easily accessible and easily applicable?

2. *Review the existing plans for their comprehensiveness and adequacy*. This review should begin by looking at the district level, then focus in on the school and building level. If there are district plans are they adequate? Do they meet the needs of the individual schools in your district, or are modifications needed? Are there supplemental individual building plans? Are those plans adequate? Sometimes, to determine the adequacy, it may be necessary to actually walk through the plan. An example of this occurred a few years ago when I was asked to evaluate a rural school crisis plan. In the process it was discovered there had been some remodeling at the school during the previous year. The crisis plan, specifically the fire response plan, had never been modified. As a result, the plan had the children exiting across the same parking lot that the fire trucks would use to enter. This was a very dangerous situation and one that could have been easily avoided if the steering committee had routinely reviewed the crisis plan for necessary modifications.

A part of the comprehensiveness of a crisis plan frequently overlooked is the availability of maps and keys. There are many types of crises where emergency service personnel need to know the *exact* layout of the building and/or need accessibility to all rooms. Provisions should be made for maps of the building to be easily and readily accessible. As a general rule, either the head secretary or head custodian will be responsible for making sure maps and/or keys are available as needed. Remember, for *every* locked door there must be a key available.

3. *Review the chain of command*: As the existing plans are reviewed, attention needs to be paid to the chain of command. Who's in charge? This is a question that may have different answers in different situations. The fundamental questions to ask in determining the chain of command should include: Who is to receive the first notification of this crisis? Who must make the immediate decisions and begin the communication process to other involved parties? This person provides the initial direction on how to proceed. Typically, this person is also the one who will coordinate response efforts. Ordinarily this will be the principal at the building level, or a district representative. Remember, it is extremely important to have one, or preferably two, people designated and trained as a backup for those times when a principal happens to be out of the building.

In some crises, where outside personnel are needed, the primary control or top level in the chain of command may pass to someone outside the building. This includes emergency situations where trained emergency personnel take charge of all the operations, either to insure physical safety or protect a "crime scene." In a situation involving the police the highest ranking officer has the ultimate responsibility. This responsibility will often be shared with either the district or school administrator. Once the physical danger has passed, the building principal or designate will again become the primary person to coordinate implementation of the crisis plan.

The person in command is heavily dependent on the rest of crisis response team members. As stated previously, it is the crisis response team that puts the steering committees' plans into action. Although, during a building crisis, the crisis response team carries the major responsibility for implementing the response plan, in some situations their task may consist primarily of coordinating the efforts of other members of the school community. It is essential that the entire building population understands successful management of any crisis is dependent upon each and every one of them.

4. *Identify members of the Crisis Response Team*: When identifying members for the crisis response team remember that membership on the crisis response team may vary from school to school, depending on available personnel. There is no required size, teams can be large or small. Generally the core response team, for each school, would include an administrative representative and at least one psychological support person (e.g., school psychologist, counselor, social worker). The rest of the members may include any combination of the following: vice principal, school nurse, certified staff representative, classified staff representative, school district representative, PTSA/PTO representative, student representative (e.g. a peer counselor or a student seen as a natural helper), community mental health agency representative, law enforcement representative, and/or community clergy representative. During a crisis every member of the staff has responsibilities and duties to perform, not just the crisis response team. If training of the staff has been thorough and complete, the actual crisis response team members simply act as decision makers and coordinators.

5. *Defining and Assigning Individual Roles*: The midst of a crisis is not the time for staff to be wondering what they should be doing. All members of the school community, from principal to custodian to parent to student, should know in advance what role is expected of them during a crisis. Defining those roles and informing each person of their role is yet another responsibility of the steering committee. Individual roles or tasks depend on the circumstances of the crisis, the

needs of the school, and the abilities/personality of the individual. However, there are some responsibilities which tend to be assigned as part of some typical job classification in a school.

- *The Principal* has the primary responsibility for overall coordination and implementation of the crisis response plan.
- *The Vice-Principal* will assist the principal and may be required to carry out all of the above functions in the absence of the principal.
- *The Chief Secretary* will receive and distribute all crisis information memos, manage the phones and may be asked to keep the "crisis log" to document what has been done during the crisis response.
- *Counselor, School Psychologist, and School Social Worker* are key member of the crisis response team. They coordinate and address the immediate and long term emotional support needs of the students and school community. Often they act as a liaison with the parents or other members of families involved in the crisis.
- *The School Nurse* will provide first aid and assist in the response as needed. S/he will assist psychological support personnel, often by providing and clarifying medical information.
- *Teachers* are responsible for the physical and emotional safety of the students. They must provide security, control possible hysteria and try to maintain sense of calm.
- *Custodians* must insure operational safety. They will also work with emergency services when necessary by providing keys, blueprints, or floor plans. They may also be helpful in monitoring the halls.

6. *Establish a Plan to Notify the School Community*: Whenever a crisis happens, notification of the school community is required. The next task for the steering is to set up plans for how that notification will take place. It seems logical that who ever receives the initial information of a crisis, or potential crisis, has the responsibility of getting that information to the principal or his/her designate. It is then the principal's decision to notify the crisis team and call them into action.

Once it has been determined by the crisis response team that a crisis response is indicated, all staff must be alerted. If it is during school hours, that notification may be done by written communication or a coded announcement. One school distributed emergency notification on a specific color paper. That color indicated the beginning of an emergency schedule. The information you want to impart includes:

- what has happened,
- what immediate responses are required,
- what information is to be given to the students,
- when the emergency staff meeting is scheduled to be held.

Crises frequently happen outside school hours. In order to insure that staff will be able to be notified after hours it is recommended that the steering committee establish an up to date *telephone tree.* Telephone trees are only as good as the information contained in them and they must be current at all times. The decision to activate the telephone tree and the content of the message to be communicated are the responsibility of the principal or his/her designate. When it be necessary to use a telephone tree it is useful to have the last person on each list call back the first person on that list. This provides confirmation that the chain was completed and the numbers are still accurate. In addition to a brief description of the crisis, the key information to impart in that phone contact is the time and place of the emergency staff meeting.

The Emergency Staff Meeting

Content of the emergency will vary, depending on the type of crisis. However, the steering committee can establish standards for this meeting. In most crises, emergency staff meetings should include the following specifics:

- detailed information about the crisis, distributed *in writing* (stating who, what, where, when, why and how),
- details of the crisis plan and how they will be applied in this situation,
- who is in charge,
- the responsibilities of each individual,
- what counseling resources are available,
- what changes will be made in the school schedule, both today and in the days ahead,
- details of the media policy,
- general information about behaviors and responses which may be expected, how to handle them and how to deal with particularly troubled students, and
- instructions on how to tell the students, if this meeting takes place before students have been informed.

Procedure for Notifying Students

A common dilemma for schools is how to inform the students. Do you make an all school P.A. announcement? Do you have a general school assembly? Or, do you have each teacher make individual classroom announcements? How can you control what is said or heard? In times of crisis, information is best shared in small, familiar, contained groups. Large groups are easily influenced by mass emotion and hysteria, and the situation may become more difficult to control. Students will turn to their teachers for support. It is important that those teachers be available to students and that the students can trust what they are being told. Experience has shown that, in most situations, the best options are to have a person (principal, counselor, or available teacher) go to each classroom to give details and to answer questions, or to have classroom teachers read the details of what has happened from a prepared "script." This insures that all the students will be given the same information at the same time. This can decrease the issues of secrets, whispers and/or rumors.

In addition to the general notification of students, it is important to consider close friends who may be more intimately affected by this particular trauma. These students may need one-on-one time to express their feelings and to talk about their reactions.

Procedure for Notifying Family and Friends

Families are also affected by a crisis in the school. This includes both the families of the student(s) directly involved and the families of the general student body. To insure family support and understanding, it is important that *all* parents in the school community must be informed of the crisis. Again, it is most helpful if this information is shared in writing. This can be done in a letter to the parents which includes:

- facts of the event,
- what is being done by the school and others,
- what behaviors they might see in their children, and
- where to turn if additional assistance is needed.

There are crisis situations, like the shooting at Hubbard Wood Elementary School, where *immediate* notification of parents is required. This can be done by phone. For a phone chain to be used, it is essential that emergency phone numbers be accurate and up-to-date. If a working relationship already exists, emergency information can also be relayed with the help of local media. Media contact, while helpful, does not take the place of direct contact by someone in the school. Even if it must take place at a later time, this contact should be made as soon as possible.

7. *Establish a Plan to Notify and Work With the Media*: Media can be both a help and a hindrance. All crisis plans must include a plan for dealing with the media. The following are general considerations for creating a media policy. Remember, the media has goals which may not compliment those of the school. Media people often believe that their primary responsibility is to "get the news." There have been times when, in pursuing this goal, they can appear intrusive by approaching everyone, including students, asking lists of seemingly insensitive questions. When four teens committed suicide in Bergenfield, New Jersey in the late 1980s, the media barrage left the other teens and the whole town feeling as though they had been used and abused in their time of grief. In one parochial elementary school, the nun who was the principal had to summon the police to stop newspersons from trying to interview kindergarten children about the murder of a classmate by her emotionally disturbed father. While it is the media's primary responsibility to get the news no matter what, it is the school's responsibility to protect the students and staff from possible abuse.

As a general rule, there should be only one media spokesperson, usually the principal, or a district designate. All questions and communication should be funneled to this spokesperson who will speak for the entire school during the crisis. This can avoid different people making contradictory statements that can only cause confusion and make it appear that the school has no clear plan of response. There should also be a back-up spokesperson in case the primary spokesperson is unavailable. Whoever serves as the spokesperson should be well-informed, able to speak effectively, have credibility in the school and community, and be clear about what s/he is and is authorized to say.

Staff and, in some cases, students should be given a prepared script that will direct media personnel back to the media spokesperson. Examples of appropriate responses might include: "I have no comment; you will need to speak to our media spokesperson," or "I have no comment; Information will be coming from our media representative." These are legitimate answers and may represent the best course of action during a crisis situation. It may also be important to say to media personnel that "Because of what has happened, we have a lot of pain right now and we need time and privacy to deal with many of these feelings. If there is information you believe you need, contact the spokesperson/principal." If you feel you can't discuss something at this time, try to explain why, if possible. A simple "no comment" is sometimes considered a red flag to media personnel.

Media personnel should not be allowed to roam freely about the school building. Decisions must be made in advance about where media should be directed. It is important to be prepared to respond if media personnel request facts describing the crisis, profiles of victims (give facts only), or photographs of victims. These are the items most frequently requested.

8. *Create an Information Bank*: Throughout a crisis and immediately follow the event(s), communication with students, staff, families, media personnel, and the general community is crucial. Because crisis situations demand that all or most attention be directed to dealing with the crisis itself, it is helpful to have pre-designated communication handouts available. For example, a page outlining children's grief responses following a death, or notes on how to respond following a suicide, could be most helpful. It may also be useful to have a general outline of a crisis letter to parents. The specific details will have to be added, however, much of that letter can be written in advance. The children's responses which parents may see, suggestions for what parents can to help their children, and resources available to parents will remain similar in most crises.

Maps of the building should be readily available to people who may need them during a crisis. Generally maps should be in the main office and the head secretary will be responsible for making them available as needed. Custodians may also have building blueprints available if needed.

9. *Plan Coordination of Staff with Identified Community Resources*: In some crisis situations it will be important and necessary to call on resources outside the school building. In some cases, additional school staff may also be necessary. The extent and severity of a crisis will determine the need for and amount of additional staff. Such staff might include substitute teachers, additional school counselors or mental health staff, or possibly additional bus drivers or telephone operators. Where will that help be found? How quickly can it be accessed? Who will make the decisions of when and whom to call?

Before hiring additional staff members, it is crucial that potential community resources are identified and that contact names and telephone numbers are made available. A list of such resources, identifying the type of agencies, services provided, names of contact people, and phone numbers should be compiled and kept in a centrally accessible place—probably both in the principal's office and with the head secretary. These resources should include such organizations/agencies as police department, fire department, ambulance units, key government officials, service agencies such as gas and electric companies, if they are effected, medical personnel, Federal Emergency Management Agency, National Guard, state emergency services, community mental health centers, psychologists, psychiatrists, thanatologists, and local religious leaders. Having these resources listed and readily accessible can save valuable time during a crisis.

10. *Establish a Debriefing Component For Each Situation*: Debriefing after a crisis is crucial. Much of this takes place within the classroom. Still, it recommended that an alternate site, outside of the classroom, be established. There are times when it is necessary to have a place for sharing and debriefing outside of a classroom after a crisis. Some students will require one-on-one time, while others will benefit from peer support groups. Libraries have been used successfully as adjuncts to counseling rooms and provide additional space for groups. Staff members also need safe places to go to express their feelings, to provide support for one another, and to draw support from community resources.

When the previous task have been completed, the steering committee is left with three final responsibilities:

1. *Creating a written crisis management plan* which includes all of the information listed above,
2. *Distributing and supporting the plan* with appropriate inservice programs, and
3. *Adopt review procedures* to be carried out on a regular, scheduled basis.

Such a review typically includes periodic reevaluation of the plan, review of all names and phone numbers contained in the plan and preparation for post-crisis evaluation. Such reviews are a critical piece of ongoing, effective crisis planning and management.

It is easy, in the aftermath of a crisis, to feel exhausted and consider the task complete. It is important, however, to reassemble both the steering committee and the crisis response team to "debrief" the crisis response, and evaluate the effectiveness of the crisis plan. The crisis response team may also need to receive counseling, using the Critical Incident Stress Debriefing Model, to deal with the stress they experienced during the event. While memories are still vivid, it has been helpful for these two groups to review the crisis plan in view of its actual implementation, to suggest needed revisions, and to recommend any additional follow-up needed for students, staff, parents, and others in the larger community.

CONCLUSION

Crises do occur! There is seldom advance warning. Successful crisis management happens only with pre-planning and preparation. These thoughts opened this chapter and it seems appropriate to end with them. Please listen and take heed to this message. Each school's leaders hold in their hands the keys necessary to insure comprehensive, successful crisis management. Use them. If your school doesn't have a steering committee, create one. Then begin a systematic evaluation and review of each of the aspects of crisis management. Don't stop until there is a written plan and all parties are prepared, knowing exactly what to do when a crisis hits your school. The future of your school, the lives and emotional well-being of students, and process of education itself may well depend on it.

REFERENCES

1. National Center for Health Statistics, *Advance Report of Final Mortality Statistics, 1990,* pre-publication copy received from the National Center for Health Statistics.
2. Burrelle's Information Services, *Transcript CBS News 60 Minutes, June 28, 1992, XXIV*:41.
3. M. Metzgar and K. Guest, *Crisis and Loss: How Can Your School Prepare?* pre-publication draft, Transition and Loss Center, Seattle Washington, June 1992.

CHAPTER 3

School Based Grief Crisis Management Programs

David K. Meagher

INTRODUCTION

The rate of sudden, unexpected violent deaths of adolescents in the United States has reached epidemic proportions. The Centers for Disease Control and Prevention have reported that almost 5000 teenagers die from non-self inflicted gun shot wounds each year. Data released by the National Center for Health Statistics corroborate this finding. Their data show that one in every four deaths among teenagers is caused by firearms and that only motor vehicle accidents account for more teen deaths. As frightening as these statistics are, it is more frightening to realize that the rate of adolescent firearm fatalities is expected to climb significantly during the 1990s. Many of these deaths are homicides and, in fact, occur on the grounds of our schools. So frequent are these events that it is now common practice to place metal detectors, the type employed by airlines to prevent firearms from being carried on board a commercial airliner, at the entrances of many inner city school buildings. So real is the threat of violence in the school that policies for searching persons entering the school building have become a standard part of the administrative routine. Yet, with all the precautions and restrictive entry policies, death still rears its ugly head inside the community.

The essence of the typical school response tends to be limited to one of the following:

- prevention of the event through technological forms of deterrence, or
- reacting to the post-event impact in a crisis fashion.

In too few instances do school planners develop and implement a comprehensive program of crisis management. The focus of effective crisis management is not intervention only. A comprehensive program of crisis management should contain three separate and distinct approaches: prevention, intervention and postvention. A description of these three components will be presented later in this chapter.

NEED FOR SCHOOL BASED DEATH CRISIS MANAGEMENT

There are perhaps no school crises as severe as those involving the death, or threatened death, of individuals linked to the school community. The gravity of developing, improving, or expanding a school based death crisis management program is embodied in the following case.

> A young high school sophomore walks toward his locker in the hallway of his school. Standing near the lockers are two classmates. The young man approaches his fellow students, removes a gun from inside his jacket and begins firing. His two classmates fall, fatally wounded from the shots as other students in the area run for cover. The young man puts the gun back inside his jacket, turns and walks slowly out of the building. The Superintendent, newly appointed and under the impression that all the schools within the system had crises intervention teams, directed that the team be mobilized. Sadly, no such team existed and the school had to rely on outside agencies and non-school personnel to provide essential services. Some questioned the efficacy of a crisis support system that asks the person in need to trust a *stranger* with personal thoughts and feelings.

Nothing can disrupt a school community as quickly as the death or impending death of a member of that community. Schools are designed, at least in theory, to be safe environments in which children are free from threat and fear and need only to concentrate on their lessons. Reality and the violence of life on the streets are not supposed to invade these learned halls. The school building is presumed to possess the same status as that of the community churches, synagogues and mosques. They are the safe havens within a community. Death must not, does not, occur within their walls. The event of death is antithetical to the functions and goals of these institutions.

Death in the school community is dealt with as a historical event; the death of historical figures or of societies. Death is always an event of the past and of the future, never of the present. However, the walls of the school are not impervious to the threats of the outside world. Death and loss do permeate the very structure and fiber of this community. Often the result of these events is the experience of a crisis either in individuals who do not possess the necessary skills for effective crisis resolution or the disruption of the normal functioning of the community brought on by the absence of any organizational crises preparedness.

Crises events, while they are unpredictable occurrences, are becoming more common and can now be expected within the community-at-large as well as in the school. A crisis management program incorporating the three aspects of prevention, intervention and postvention requires a great deal of organizational planning and development to achieve the goal of creating and maintaining necessary resources and services that will provide all affected individuals with the best opportunity to engage in constructive coping behaviors.

DEFINITIONS

A *crisis* is defined as a serious or decisive state of things. In terms of an individual or group, crisis is an acute, emotional upset arising from situational, developmental, or social sources and resulting in a temporary inability to cope through usual problem solving devices [1].

Hoff differentiates between "crisis" and "emergency" [2]. *Emergency,* according to Hoff, is not crisis, it is an unforseen combination of circumstances that call for immediate action, often with life and death implications. Crisis occur when a person's inability to cope with an event such as an emergency leads to an experience of stress that is so severe that s/he cannot find relief. It is important to understand that stress is not crisis, it is a *symptom* of crisis. *Stress* is the tension or pressure that is felt when one is in crisis. *Crisis management* is defined as a process in which all the aspects of working through a crisis are utilized to the point of crisis elimination, resolution or prevention.

Hoff and Miller define *crisis counseling* and *crisis intervention* as essential components of the crisis management process [1].

Crisis counseling is an aspect of the crisis management process focusing particularly on the emotional ramifications of the crisis. The person who engages in crisis counseling must be one who has formal preparation in counseling techniques.

Crisis intervention is defined as that aspect of the management process that focuses on the resolution of the immediate problem through the use of personal, social, environmental, and sometimes material resources.

Crisis prevention is the process of reducing the onset of acute, emotional upset experienced in a crisis by developing educational programs that enable a person to examine her/his coping behaviors, resources and skill of assessment [1]. The focus of crisis prevention programs is on eliminating those controllable causative factors which would prevent the onset of the series of one or more necessary elements of a crisis or strengthening or expanding the options perceived as available when one is engaged in decision making. A significant crisis prevention program that may be incorporated into a school program is death education.

Crisis postvention is defined as a process of, for the lack of a better illustration, damage assessment and damage control. Postvention programs attempt to assess the consequence of a resolved crisis experience on the ability of the person to continue to function. It is a process of assisting the person to learn how to live with the aftermath and all its effects. A recommendation to participate in long term counseling is an example of the postvention process.

The loss of someone due to death is regarded as a critical life event which may disturb an individual's emotional equilibrium. As such, it may create extreme difficulty in the affected individual's ability to function within relationships and to accomplish necessary tasks. These potentials are consistent with a crisis syndrome [3]. However, the origins of the crisis are significantly different than those of non-death crises so that usual crisis intervention procedures may not be effective when applied. One may need to engage in *grief crisis intervention,* a process that employs grief counseling techniques with selected crisis intervention procedures.

Crises resulting from sudden, unexpected and violent events compound the stress experienced as it severely weakens the communal sense of security and safety. The school community, like any organization or society, must not wait until a crisis occurs to initiate the development of a crisis support program. There is a need for program planning that involves everyone on the staff, from the top of the organizational ladder, the principal, to every rung of the structure. This includes the custodial staff and, yes, even members of the transportation unit. Program planning must not be limited to the usual form of reactive response, crisis intervention, but must include the other two essential component of the necessary triad of crises support; prevention and postvention strategies.

The parameters of the impact of crisis are not always limited to the school grounds or to the school personnel as illustrated in the following case.

> Two classes from an elementary school are on a field trip that the children looked forward to for many months. They were going to visit the observation deck on the 108th floor of one of the twin towers of the World Trade Center in New York City. Arriving in the mid-morning, the classes waited for available space on the elevators that would take them to what is often described as the windows of the world. The first class had arrived at the observation deck and, with their teachers, were awaiting the arrival of the second class. As the children in the second class were ascending in the elevator car that would take them to the heavens, a bomb exploded in the subterranean parking lot of the building, causing all power to be shut off and dense, choking smoke to rise through the shafts and stairwells of the tower. One class is trapped within the dark confines of the elevator car. The other group is restricted to the observation deck with no safe egress as the street is 108 floors below, the stairwells are filled with thick smoke, the elevators are not working and snow is falling preventing rescue helicopters from landing on the roof helicopter pad. It is more than six hours before emergency personnel are able to reach the children and escort them and the teachers to safety. During this time the parents of the children congregate in the school auditorium watching television reports of the disaster and praying for the safe return of their children.

The safe return of these children does not end the experience for them, their parents, or their teachers. The crisis does not disappear with the passing out of souvenir tee shirts with the message, "I Survived The Twin Tower Terror" embossed on the front. The crisis that a disaster of this nature produces is not limited only to the affected children and their parents, but includes the rest of the school community, children and staff, as well as the other parents and guardians whose children are not on the field trip and may be safely ensconced in the school building as the event unfolds.

PLANNING CRISIS MANAGEMENT PROGRAMS

The idea of planning a crisis management program is more than a recommendation, it is a responsibility of the whole staff: administrators, faculty, and others, who should be willing to be involved in the development of a comprehensive crisis support program designed to assist all members of the community. The tasks principals and administrators need to accomplish include the development and adherence to a requirement that all the counseling programs within a school are prepared to respond immediately to a crisis. There is a need for a *written* protocol to incorporate the plan into the school or district policy. This protocol should include:

1. the identification of the individual(s) who is responsible for the provision of service;
2. a description of the recommended qualifications a crisis intervener, including a description of the type of academic work and clinical experience desired of someone assuming this role;
3. the types of crises which would necessitate the activation of the plan and personnel;
4. a plan of evaluation for:
   a. follow-up to initial support,
   b. effectiveness of the intervention, and
5. the identification of the school or district person to whom all support personnel are accountable.

THE CRISIS TEAM

The members of the crisis team need to be identified and need to be in place from the first day of the school year. The school administration cannot wait until a crisis such as the one described at the beginning of this chapter to occur before creating and assembling a crisis team. Questions concerning the make-up of the team that need to be considered are:

1. should the team be comprised of school personnel only?
2. what other community agencies might be enlisted to provide personnel on a need basis?
3. how many crisis team members should there be?
4. what should the function of this team be?

Most, if not all, of these questions cannot be answered definitively. The policy of the school vis-a-vis the inclusion of non-school personnel in a crisis situation, the availability of non-school agencies and trained personnel and the size of the school budget are just a few variables that will influence the responses to these questions.

The answer to the question of who will be a member of the team will depend on what skills and knowledge are considered necessary prerequisites for being a team member. *It should not be assumed that the education and training a school counselor/psychologist receives automatically prepares her/him to adequately assist in a death related crisis.* A death related crisis causes a grief crisis to develop. A death related crisis is one brought on by the death of a student or other member of the school community due to an illness or accident as well as death brought on by more violent and sudden causes: suicide, murder, or other types of catastrophes. Most school psychology and counseling preparation programs focus in their training on the identification of learning problems and the response to behavioral problems that may be displayed by students. Even where a school psychologist and/or counselor may have some competency in grief support, her/his services are generally available only to the student population. Administrators, faculty, and other staff are left to their own resources in trying to identify and secure some supportive services. Parents of the students are, likewise, usually not afforded the support they may need. Members of the community-at-large are most certainly disenfranchised when a determination is being made as to who will be offered support services by the school crisis team. School planners may fail to recognize that the events that occur within the school community are carried out of the building to the home and acted out by the children. The failure to recognize a relationship between what occurs within the school and the events in the greater society and the inability to recognize the validity of the grief being experienced by individuals having no direct contact with the schools create the disenfranchisement of those persons in the acknowledgment of a communal grief response and of the provision of any grief support services [4].

Sometimes when the door is opened even slightly, the material contained within the room that has piled up over the years, may come tumbling down in the fashion of a comedy routine. I became acutely aware of this potential in the following experience.

I received an invitation by the school psychologist at an area elementary school to speak with some of the parents of the fourth grade children. I was informed by the psychologist that one of the children in the class had recently experienced the death of a newborn sibling. This child brought many of his questions and concerns into the classroom. The teacher was not prepared to deal with the child's concerns, nor was she ready for the impact this event seemed to be having on the other children in the class. Many of the children brought their own questions and fears home and placed them onto their parents. This series of circumstances began to snowball as the parents were at a loss on how to deal with their children's questions and concerns. The school psychologist, who initially tried to explain to the parents that their children's responses were normal and would pass with time, found the parents expressing frustration, a sense of inadequacy, and serious concern about the support they and their children were receiving.

After I sat for a short time with some twenty parents, all of them mothers, it became apparent to me that they were not discussing only the death of this particular fourth grader's sibling but were bringing to the meeting their own previously unresolved losses which they realized were interfering with the way in which they were or were not able help their own children. The school psychologist had not spent a great deal of time in her own academic preparation or training focusing on how to deal with the crisis of death. It had been discussed as a very minor component within a larger presentation of crisis intervention.

PREPARATION OF STAFF

Training

A school counselor or school psychologist needs to receive training as a grief counselor, especially in grief crisis counseling. This training should include:

1. an examination of one's own death related concerns and issues;
2. understanding the grief process, especially with a focus on the initial phases of grief and the long term manifestations of unresolved grief; and
3. becoming familiar with the research in disenfranchised grief, complicated grief and pathological grief.

The teacher needs to understand death and children. In addition, the teacher needs to know what his/her roles are in relation to the crisis intervention team.

An educational program designed to train individuals to do crisis counseling, especially crisis grief counseling, should include the following three areas:

- knowledge,
- attitudes, and
- skills.

The essential concepts the crisis counselor/intervener should possess include:

- knowledge of crisis theory and principles of crisis management;
- a familiarity with the discipline of suicidology;
- knowledge of victimology;
- a study of death attitudes and concerns, the dying process and grief work;

- a working understanding of the principles of communication;
- familiarity with relevant ethical and legal issues; and
- an understanding of team relationships in crisis work.

Attitudes

Whether one is involved in prevention or intervention, the person needs to have a good understanding of her/his attitudes. The attitudes one would hope would be present in the crisis worker are:

- an acceptance of an non-judgmental response to persons different from self and toward controversial issues—not discussing the moral rightness or wrongness of abortion with a person;
- a balanced, realistic attitude toward oneself in the helper role—not expecting to rescue or save everyone whom one assists;
- a realistic and humane approach to death, dying and self-destructive behavior;
- being able to deal with emotional issues like AIDS; and
- a coming to terms with one's own feelings about death, dying and loss.

Skills

In the area of skills, it would be advantageous for both the crisis worker and for the person with whom one is working if the crisis support person:

1. is able to apply the techniques of formal crisis management including the skills of assessment, planning, implementation, and evaluation;
2. possesses good communication skills including the ability to listen actively, question discretely, respond empathetically, and advise and direct appropriately;
3. is able to mobilize community resources effectively and efficiently; and
4. is able to keep accurate records.

INTERVENTION

A strategy for activating the crisis intervention component of the management process must include: ways in which the onset of a crisis is detected and made known; a procedure for putting the intervention program into action; and a process of assessment of the crisis, identification of those in need and of their specific needs.

Delivery of Crisis Services

The delivery of crisis services involves four essential steps that characterize the crisis management process:

1. an assessment of the crisis;
2. the development of a plan based on assessment data,
3. a way of implementing the plan, and
4. a program of follow-up and evaluation [1].

Goals of Grief Crisis Intervention

The goals of a grief crisis intervention program include:

1. the provision of support to those of the educational community when a member dies;
2. the ability to acknowledge the death of the community member and affirm the life of the survivors;
3. the provision of an organized, systemic, but flexible approach to dealing with tragedy;
4. the ability to demonstrate that the grieving process is a natural part of the total human response following any loss;
5. the provision of time so as to permit one to reflect on the significance of that member to the school;
6. the allowing of the school to make a tangible response to defend immediate survivors on behalf of the school;
7. the giving of consolation and comfort to the group; and
8. the creation of effective follow-up resources forsurvivors, as needed [5].

A major limitation on the provision of usual grief counseling services is related to the place and time opportunities. The hours of operation and the mission and purposes of the school do not easily accommodate the provision of grief counseling services when the need might arise in the students or other affected persons. Competing services and programs for the space and resources within the school make it very difficult to offer grief counseling support. These limitations create a greater need to develop effective grief *crisis* counseling. This procedure usually involves more of a surviving the immediate acute loss response than the longer term assistance of helping the individual achieve a completion of all grief tasks. The latter is part of grief counseling.

PREVENTION AS A PART OF MANAGEMENT

As was stated earlier, crises are unpredictable. One may be able to prepare for an expected death of a loved one but preparing for major disasters and sudden death are difficult if not impossible. This, however, does not mean that no attempts at prevention are planned. Hoff suggests three types of crisis prevention potentials which are equivalent to the earlier designations of prevention, intervention and postvention:

1. *primary prevention (prevention)* which occurs in educational and consultative programs;
2. *secondary prevention (intervention)* which involves the attempts to shorten the time the crisis is impacting the individual; and
3. *tertiary prevention (postvention)* which is a process designed to reduce the disabling effects of the crisis experience [2].

Primary Prevention

The first part of a program of prevention (primary prevention) is the development of curricula offerings that provide an opportunity for students to examine and assess coping skills. These curricula offerings should be courses taught by faculty who possess the necessary educational background to conduct classes in death, dying, suicide, grief resolution, and coping with crises.

Secondary Prevention

Secondary prevention, apart from the actual application of crisis intervention techniques in counseling an individual, involves the establishment of a program of support and the process of putting the program into operation when needed. This planning for prevention must include the development of a set of minimal education/training standards that must absolutely be required of the individual who will most be involved with primary prevention, the teacher of death education.

School Mental Health Providers

Educational training programs for school mental health providers (school psychologists or counselors) should include and examination of, or experience in:

1. the process and techniques of crisis intervention;
2. children and death;
3. an introductory course in death and dying; and
4. a course on grief counseling.

Competencies of Crisis Interveners

The essential competencies for grief crisis interveners and death educators are:

1. *Knowledge of self*—the ability to come to terms with one's feelings and to be aware of their influence on the individual's total personality.
2. *Knowledge of the subject matter*—the need to know the appropriate subject matter the counselor will be called upon to assist or the educator is to teach.
3. *Knowledge of communication skills*—the ability to use the language of death easily and naturally, especially in the presence of the young.
4. *Knowledge of the student*—the need to be familiar with the sequence of psychothanatological developmental events throughout life and to have a sympathetic understanding of common problems associated with them.
5. *Knowledge of the total environment*—a need to be acutely aware of the enormous social changes that are in progress and their impact on the patterns of attitudes, practices, laws, and institutions concerning crises and death.
6. *Knowledge of the principles of curriculum design*—the ability to effectively organize a curriculum in death education; to know how to construct a curriculum that is logical and developmental in its design.
7. *Knowledge of what is possible in the classroom*—the ability to develop appropriate behavioral objectives in the cognitive, affective and behavioral domains and the ability to integrate these domains with each other.

Preparation of Death Educators

Education programs for death educators should go further and include some preparation for being a death educator. This preparation should examine the following areas of concern.

Components of Responsible Death Education

1. A study of the emotional and social needs of students at various age levels.
2. An examination of the needs of society for adequately informed children and youth.
3. The development of an understanding of the significant areas of influence such as the home, community, religion and the media.

Preparation to Teach Death Education

1. Personal preparation: examination of personal knowledge, feelings, attitudes, values, and the sources of conviction and biases.
2. Professional preparation:
   a. understanding the teaching role as: a conveyor of information, a resource person, a motivator and director, and counselor;
   b. understanding the process of evaluation of current literature in death, philosophies, curricula, methods and materials, audio-visual aids, and the implications of new directions in behavior, attitudes, family living and morality
   c. understanding and presenting concepts and using materials: utilizing student knowledge and experience, counteracting misinformation, fielding sensitive questions, dealing with students personal concerns, and utilizing resource people.

Program Development and Coordination

1. Development of effective methods of determining community needs and interests.
2. Program planning: working with various community organizations, parents and other school programs to create a maximum effective support for all affected persons in and away from the school environment.
3. Orienting school staff: the development of in-service programs and the integration of death education with other subject areas.
4. Dealing with controversy in death education: understanding how to address issues such as physician-assisted suicide, and right to die issues.

THE EXTENT OF INFLUENCE

When a crisis occurs away from the school or during times that the school is not in session, administrators may fail to recognize it as a legitimate event of concern. Under the belief that one is protecting others by not allowing them to learn of the crisis precipitating event, information may be withheld. It is a perpetuation of the myth that maintains what you do not know will not hurt you. But, the reality is that eventually truth will out and the intensity of the crisis may be compounded by the covert deception that is inherent in the withholding of information. The following case illustrates the consequence of such deception.

Susan W., a Middle School English teacher, died in an automobile accident on a Friday afternoon as she was driving out of state to visit her parents. Hit head on by a young man who was speeding and who lost control of his car, the medical examiner described the death as instantaneous. Although Susan W. was a very popular teacher, well liked by both her students and colleagues, most people in the town were not aware of her death when school resumed on Monday morning. Her death principal, uncertain about how to deal with this tragedy, hired a substitute to teach her classes. Susan's students asked the substitute to explain why their regular teacher was not there. The substitute did not have any knowledge of Susan's death and assumed that Susan was sick. This is what she conveyed to the students. As the school day drew to a close, the principal announced the news of Susan's death over the PA system to all the classes. It was expected that dismissal would follow the announcement. Instead of the usual student rush to exit the building, an acute silence settled over the building as students and staff sat in shock. Some minutes later, many of Susan's students sought out the substitute and angrily demanded to know why she had lied to them. The substitute teacher felt she was manipulated by the principal for not informing her of the reason why Susan was not at work. Susan's colleagues, many of whom considered themselves her friends, experienced severe depression and confusion about what they should now do. It was some time before the school was able to return to a resemblance of its previous environmental state as a center of learning.

A response to this crisis should have included:

1. making the facts of the event known to all appropriate persons (faculty, staff, students and substitute teachers) in a sensitive and caring way—the usual methods of making announcements or disseminating information should *not* be employed;
2. controlling the spread of rumors about the cause of the death and the effect of the event on the remains of the deceased—the belief that the remains of the deceased suffered intense physical destruction may result in a feeling of additional loss within those who knew and cared for Susan and who have not had a great deal experience with death;
3. planning for the inclusion of students in scheduled mourning rituals, preparing the student to participate, plan for the possibility of having to provide emotional assistance to students during their participation and/ or allowing for the school community to plan its own memorial and or mourning activities;

4. providing grief support services to all members of the community who may be in need of, or wish, assistance, including the provision of services to the grief crisis interveners;
5. referring to non-school services when necessary and appropriate;
6. assessing the effectiveness of the process, including evaluation by recipients of support service, and revising where necessary; and
7. scheduling a follow-up assessment of the needs and behaviors of the members of the school community.

SUMMARY

In summary, a list of suggested guidelines for a school based grief crisis management program should include:

- confront—do not attempt to deny or avoid the crisis, the problem will not disappear on its own;
- prepare in anticipation—do not prepare in crisis;
- develop inclusive support programs—do not create policies of exclusion;
- seek qualified personnel—do not appoint untrained people;
- modify protocol based on assessment and evaluation of process and not on the unsubstantiated perceptions of a few; and
- include care for the crisis team members as part of the planned support program—do not assume that the caregiver needs no care.

REFERENCES

1. L. A. Hoff and N. Miller, *Programs for People in Crisis,* Northeastern University Custom Book Program, Boston, 1987.
2. L. A. Hoff, *People in Crisis,* Addison-Wesley Publishing Company, Menlo Park, California, 1984.
3. G. Burnell and A. L. Burnell, *Clinical Management of Bereavement,* Human Sciences Press, New York, 1988.
4. K. J. Doka, *Disenfranchised Grief,* Lexington Books, Lexington, Massachusetts, 1989.
5. S. L. Cobb, Guideline for Dealing with Traumatic Events in the School Community, in *The Dying and The Bereaved Teenager,* John D. Morgan, (ed.), The Charles Press, Philadelphia, 1990.

CHAPTER 4

The Role of the School Nurse in Crises

Eileen P. Stevenson

A school nurse has an opportunity to create an environment in the school health office so that, on a regular basis, it can be seen by school staff, students, and their families as a "safe place." It can be a haven where, in addition to medical aid, a person (whether student, staff member, or parent) can find quiet, privacy, comfort, and a sympathetic ear. In addition, the nurse can refer students for special help or assist an individual with information and/or contact persons who can offer support. The nurse/educator is seen as a teacher, a health professional, a resource person, and at times assumes the role of counselor or confidant. In time of crisis each of these roles comes into play.

The school nurse has a unique opportunity to get to know students. Because nursing is viewed as a *caring* profession, it is a reasonable assumption on the student's part to expect some extra caring from her/him. Generally, students first view the nurse's office in a *neutral* fashion. Some of the emotional barriers that are present in the classroom are absent in the health office.

If a nurse puts paperwork or procedure before the needs of the individual student, barriers may be placed between nurse and student that block later communication. If the health office has a sterile, medicinal atmosphere it may remind some students of past experiences with treatment for illness or of hospitalization. This makes a positive interaction less likely. At the same time, too serious a demeanor on the part of a school nurse, the "Nurse Ratchet" look, can cause a child to not even approach the nurse at times of emotional distress. If we allow this to happen, we lose a great opportunity to be of real help to students facing crises.

With all of the pressures that today's young people face, they need a place where they can go when those pressures may be too much. A caring school nurse can make the office into just such a *safe place* for each student. Because the nurse usually sees students on a one-to-one basis there is less of a need for "defenses." It is easier to touch and to talk when it is just "you and me," rather than "you, me and twenty-five others."

The nurse has an opportunity to get to know the whole child and not just the "student." There is nothing academic which the child must prove to the nurse: no test scores, no recitation, etc. In most cases the nurse is not compelled to make judgements regarding the student's ability of behavior. This allows student and nurse to get to know one another on a more personal level. If this relationship is important to students on a daily basis, it is of even greater importance in a time of crisis.

To create this safe place takes *time*. The needed level of trust develops slowly. The nurse must be available to students, both in and out of the office, and must get to know students as individuals, calling them by name in the halls or lunchroom or, in the case of younger children, on the playground. S/he should seek to inject his/her personality into the office, through artwork, "collections" (nurse statues, toys, dolls, etc.), colorful privacy screen, or plants (a touch of nature/life). The office should be distinctively "his/hers." As long as it does not disrupt their classes, the students should feel free to visit the office for even small complaints, or just to say, "Hi." A nurse who seeks to develop this type of relationship with students must be willing to help students, deal with affective (emotional) issues which confront them.

A school nurse cannot, and should never seek to, *replace* a parent. However, our schools are charged to act *in loco parentis* (in place of parents) and, in many cases, the school nurse becomes the caring adult needed by children when in our schools.

Recognizing the special role of the school nurse, a number of contingency plans, such as the River Dell Protocol, have used the nurse's office as a focal point for helping students to cope with emotional upheavals in their lives. The River Dell Protocol, which was distributed nationwide by the National Association of Secondary School Principals, recommended that the nurse not be assigned to go to classes to deliver the news to students of a death, because s/he was too valuable to be unavailable to the majority of students in a time of crisis [1].

When the nurse acts as "counselor" and confidant for the students, it means his/her responsibilities will be greatly expanded. If the nurse accepts this expanded definition of his/her role, s/he must be willing to intercede for his/her charges and to act as an advocate on their behalf. To be able to act as an effective support for students in times of crisis, a nurse must expand his/her professional background and training to include: crisis intervention and crisis resolution, an understanding of the dynamics of the grief process, and techniques of counseling and Critical Incident Stress Debriefing. Not ever school nurse will wish to accept this added responsibility. A nurse who takes the time and makes the effort to prepare for crises can be a resource to the nursing colleagues who may not have similar preparation or interest.

The chief responsibility of the school nurse is to care for the health and welfare of the students and staff. Physical needs can be cared for in a professional manner that is, at the same time, emotionally distant. This requires intellectual and physical involvement, but not an emotional investment. Before the nurse can help students and staff to deal with their losses and grief, s/he must deal with his/her own emotional baggage. S/he must be able to acknowledge the losses and pain of his/her own past to be truly open to the emotional needs of others.

CREATING A SAFE HAVEN

Some students need only a safe place to take "time-out" from the pressures of life. As their somatic complaints are being addressed, they sometimes give clues to their emotional concerns. If their physical needs have been addressed in a caring, concerned way, they can begin to see the nurse's office as a place where they can vent their emotions without fear of being judged.

How this is done will vary with each individual (student or nurse). Each school nurse has discretion in the running of their office. State mandates give more screenings, more forms and more state reports, so much so that, at times, a school nurse may be faced with the choice of completing paperwork or helping an individual child. In some schools this can mean choosing between caring for *all* the needs of students and keeping one's job. At times like this, an understanding administrator can be the key individual who can help the nurse to strike that critical balance which will allow time for *both* administrative record keeping and caring for the needs of students and staff.

As the resident health care specialist in most schools, the school nurse is often the liaison between home and school in matters of serious illness, death, and/or grief. Often, the fears of children in regard to these issues are without foundation and merely talking to the nurse can help to reduce anxiety. When these issues become real, his/her knowledge can be a comfort to the child, to family members and to concerned staff. Anxious or upset students may be offered a safe place to talk about their feelings, or just to sit and have a quiet moment. Listening to soft music or recordings of nature sounds, such as waves or the wind in the woods, can have a soothing effect on children. Then, they may be able to speak about their particular concerns. The school nurse must be aware of the limits that exist on the help that can be offered directly. However, s/he does not need to act alone and must be willing and able to draw on the other personnel within the school system and in the greater community, if the need should arise.

Our school system was recently forced to confront the issues surrounding the sudden death of a student. A sixth grade student was struck by a car on a Saturday and died instantly. Our school housed fourth and fifth grade students. The boy who had died was a student in another school in our district, but he was known to all of the teachers and he had a younger sibling in our school. Implementing a school emergency plan, the principal used the emergency phone list to notify each of the staff members. On Monday morning, half an hour before school opened, there was a faculty meeting to discuss what would be done. At the regular opening exercises, the principal announced that the boy had been killed suddenly and that we would take a moment of silence to remember him. Students who knew the young man were asked to think of a special quality of his which they admired, while those who had not really known him were asked to remember someone whose friendship they were thankful for. The students were then told by the principal that they could ask any questions they had during the day of their teachers. Or, if they wished, they could seek answers to their questions from the principal or from the school nurse.

Students did avail themselves of this opportunity and many of them wished to speak to the school nurse. Their questions and concerns were very down to earth. They asked:

- What is a wake?
- What is a casket?
- Do I have to look at the casket?
- What should I wear?
- How should I act?
- What should I say to his parents?

Simple, straight-forward answers were provided for each of these questions.

- A wake is a chance to say goodbye to someone who has died. It is a chance for everyone to show how he/she feels about this death and to show how special the person was who died.
- A casket is a box which holds the body of a dead person. If it would bother you, you do not have to "look." There is no need for you do anything that you do not feel you can do.
- Wear something which you believe would show respect. Some people might wear a shirt and tie, or a dress or your best outfit. (For the boy who asked the question, it was a sweat suit. It was the best he had and it was fine.)
- Just talk about what you remember about the young man who died. Sharing your memories about him with others who loved him is a special gift at this difficult time.

There are a number of possible explanations for the large number of questions brought to the school nurse. Students repeatedly expressed concern for the parents of the student who had died. It is possible that this concern was transferred to their own parents because most of these youngsters did not speak about the death or ask questions at home, unless first encouraged to do so by their parents. The children appeared to be trying to avoid doing or saying anything which would cause their parents to be sad or to worry. The children said they were less nervous about talking to the nurse because they saw her/him as someone who had helped people with these issues before. Even though there was a close relationship between nurse and students, the young people could still maintain some "distance" because the nurse was not *their* parent.

TEACHER CONCERNS

The teachers in the school cooperated with, and supported, the efforts of the principal but they too experienced a wide range of reactions. Some teachers needed reassurance that what they were doing with their students was *right*. Teachers who could deal effectively with the intellectual aspects of the situation, or answered factual questions with little difficulty, were afraid of making a mistake when dealing with affective concerns or issues related to grief-related emotions. They were willing to ease up on the academic requirements placed on students in the wake of the death, but they were concerned that they might be enabling the child to use the grief process in a harmful way . . . to "take advantage" of the situation. Staff members were concerned that students who were not dealing at the time with serious emotional issues might say that they were in order to take time out from class or to receive special attention.

When student visits to the principal and to the nurse continued for several days after their schoolmate's death, teachers wanted to know if this was permissible and if it was "normal." They asked if they should allow students to continue to do this. Teachers were reassured that this was allowed. Most of the students simply wanted to talk about their feelings and some had a question they needed to ask. If access to a caring listener had been denied, the resulting anxiety could have made "normal" learning difficult or impossible. The teachers wanted to help their students. They just wanted to be sure that this way the right way to be of help. In this case, the nurse becomes a resource and support for teachers. S/he can provide explanation, clarification and support for their efforts on behalf of their students. Teachers are correct in their perception that with an issue which generates such strong emotions, there may be risks. Some students may encounter difficulties which require interventions that are beyond the ability of the immediate school staff members. What should a teacher do and what should be referred to other support personnel? Any attempt to help a troubled students can carry with it the "risk" of generating even stronger feelings on the part of the student. It is a role of the school nurse to help the teacher decide what "risks" are justified.

"JUSTIFIED" RISK?

When dealing with the emotions of students there is, even in the best of school settings, an issue of risk that must be considered. There are many sources which state that it is no longer "safe" for teachers or staff members to touch students. It is a matter of public record that in an average year in the State of New Jersey there are over 100 cases of alleged child abuse pending against educators. The majority of these cases are eventually found to have no basis for prosecution of the individual(s) involved. Whether or not these cases are dismissed, or lead to prosecution and the accused is found to be not guilty, the damage has already been done. In every case, a career and a life have been permanently effected. Even when there is no substance found, it will appear on the educator's record for many years that this person was *accused* of child abuse.

The school nurse cannot avoid *touching* his/her charges both physically and emotionally. It must be remembered that there is a line between *good* touching and *bad* touching and that even young children should be made aware of what this means. It is the nurse who is often appointed to be the person who must explain this difference to students. An unfounded charge can be leveled at *any* individual, whether they have, in fact, touched a student or not. As was the case with striking a balance between bureaucratic paperwork and personal care, this issue is one which must be addressed individually by each school nurse. The nurse must be prepared to live with the consequences of his/her choice, whatever they may be. The time to make such a determination is not in the midst of a crisis. As with other important decisions concerning crisis intervention, this is a choice which is best made prior to a crisis, when there is time for calm reflection on each of the possible consequences.

A PLAN OF ACTION FOR THE SCHOOL NURSE

For the office of the school nurse to effectively assist students during a crisis, there should be a plan in place which includes the follow steps:

- Create a network of nurses from the school system and other systems, to choose from a variety of professional opinions and mutual support in times of crisis.
- Create a plan to address the physical needs of each student and do so in a caring, supportive way. Since some situations may well involve large numbers of students, the nurse should also have a plan in place which will allow him/her to draw on the resources of the community as a whole and to coordinate the efforts of a number of people. This may well include both health care professionals and volunteers.
- Develop personal listening skills in order to learn the concerns of students, both spoken and unspoken, which may follow a traumatic episode.
- Open channels of communication with administrators, staff members, parents and community resources, and, when possible, seek the support of each of these groups for all planned actions.
- Examine personal issues which may remain for the nurse so that these do not interfere with his/her ability to be alert to and help students deal with their present pain and concerns.

When I arrived at my school, when students were to be punished they were sent to the nurse's office. However, students soon began to look for reasons to come to the office to "talk about life." They just wanted to discuss their problems and concerns. Ultimately, it is the students who will tell the school nurse if his/her office is seen as a safe haven. They are the final judges of the effectiveness of any such plan. If a nurse's office is such a place it will be able to serve as a logical focal point in times of crisis for the medical aspects of intervention efforts on behalf of students. If it is not already seen in this light, it will be most difficult to change student perceptions during and/or after a crisis occurs.

REFERENCE

1. R. G. Stevenson and H. L. Powers, How to Handle Death In the School, *TIPS for Principals from NAASP*, December 1986.

BIBLIOGRAPHY

Fassler, J., *Helping Children Cope*, Free Press, New York, 1978.

Kavanaugh, R. E., Children's Special Needs, in *Dealing With Death and Dying*, P. Chaney (ed.), Nursing 78 Books, Horsham, Pennsylvania, 1980.

Lochner, C., Helping Ourselves to Help Others, *Archives of the Foundation of Thanatology, 14*:1, 1987.

Schaefer, D. and C. Lyons, *How Do We Tell the Children?* Newmarket Press, New York, 1986.

CHAPTER 5

Religious Education as an Aid in Crisis Intervention

Rabbi Daniel A. Roberts

> You are with us in our prayer, in our love and our doubt, in our longing to feel Your presence and do Your will. You are the still, clear voice within us. Therefore, O God, when doubt troubles us, when anxiety makes us tremble, and pain clouds the mind, we look inward for the answer to our prayers. There may we find You, and there find courage, insight, and endurance [1, p. 329].

In one sense, handling a crisis in a religious school setting is no different from handling a crisis in a public school. For both the welfare of the student as well as the institution, a crisis must be addressed because, if ignored, it will fester and become infected. In another sense, handling crises in a religious setting is different, for resolving trauma is what religion does best and in reality is the *sine qua non* of religious education. What follows are some ideas of how Jewish education can and should address the issue of coping with crisis. The ideas can be easily extrapolated by those of other religions to fit any religious school setting.

INTRODUCTION

Crisis represents the disruption of the equilibrium of normal daily living, or as Gerald Caplan defines it, "an upset in a steady state" [2, p. 24]. If, therefore crisis means insecurity, peril, threat of destruction, obstacles to life goals, or feeling helpless for being out of control, then, in reality, all of life consists of either "minor" or "major" crises. Be it the trauma precipitated by changes in the normal course of living, such as entry into school, birth of a sibling, becoming an adolescent, marriage, retirement, or death, or those occasioned by accidental hazardous events, such as acute or chronic illness, accidents, war, famine, death of a leader, or family dislocations [3, pp. 424-425], ultimately people must be empowered to use one of God's gifts to humanity—the ability to cope with the variations and changing patterns of life. Although a crisis experience attunes us to the very issues which religion addresses (the meaning of life, an appreciation of its transitory nature, and the unjust realities of life's experiences), it is religion, through ritual, prayer, stories, tradition, customs, and hope, that gives us a rock on which to stand so that we can confront tomorrow.

Roger Schmidt, in *Exploring Religion*, explains it well.

> Religious beliefs, practices, and communities have been the primary systems of meaning through which ultimate situations and concerns are integrated into a vision of the whole of reality. They are supportive systems that help humans live through their suffering, face death with equanimity, and understand (if only dimly) who they are, why they are, and what they can hope for. As Clifford Geertz observed, 'The problem of suffering is, paradoxically, not how to avoid suffering, but how to make physical pain, personal loss, worldly defeat, or the helpless contemplation of others' agony something bearable, supportable . . .' [4, p. 94].

Through religion people often find meaning when all of life seems to be against them, discover hope when life seems hopeless, find strength when anxiety makes them tremble and pain clouds the mind. It is ritual prayer and community that supports people when they are in their greatest hour of need. "If you grow up in a family with strong rituals," writes Dr. Steven J. Wolin, a psychiatrist at the Family Research Center at George Washington University and a leader in research on family rituals, "you're more likely to be resilient as an adult" [5]. Results of a survey of 240 college students and seventy of their parents indicate that having meaningful family rituals gives students a more positive self-image and enables them to better deal with the pressure of freshman year [5]. In her best-selling book, *Pathfinders*, Gail Sheehy states that the ability to pray is one of the four coping devices that "Pathfinders," people who overcome life's crises, use as protection against change and uncertainty. The other three coping devices are more work, dependence on friends, and humor [6, p. 88]. "Prayer," writes Rabbi Zvi Yehuda, is "one of the ways by which man seeks to formalize and concretize his constant search for meaning and understanding. Prayer demonstrates man's inquisitive exploration of, and perplexing marvel at the unknown dimensions of existence;

expressing thereby man's concern with the sublime, the inexplicable, and the unreachable in his life" [7].

During moments of crisis we feel most alone, vulnerable, helpless, and out of control. We most desperately seek what religion has to offer: an outside authority that stabilizes, calms, and gives us a sense of hope that tomorrow *will be* a better day and there is a God who cares. We need to know that our friends are there for us, and that we are still loved despite all that has happened to us. When crises overcome us, especially the reality of our own mortality, life threatening illness, or the death of someone close to us, we search for what religion offers: the ability to gain control over our experiences. Ritual, hope, and vision of a world to come calm and stabilize us so that we are able to pick up the pieces and deal with the realities of life. The beauty of religious tradition is that it offers us not just one coping mechanism but a variety of responses to crisis: social and emotional support, a broader vista on the incident, and hope for future change.

Since this nation prides itself on a division of church and state, and since secularism has so sterilized our educational system that public school educators tremble to speak of anything which involves morals and values, it is the premise of this chapter that religious school can offer far more in helping young people cope with crises than can the public schools. Religious school should not just be a place where students learn history, customs, or the Hebrew language, but should be an institution where they learn how to use ritual, prayer, community, and faith to wrestle with life's crises. Historical events will not wed a young person to his religion; however, the vivid memories of how his religion and friends supported and cared for him in an hour of need will do so. A religious experience which has aided a youth to confront a traumatic event will positively affect his bond with Judaism. Indeed, the great educator John Dewey posits that people learn best when the learning grows out of and addresses their genuine concerns and problems [8, p. 79].

If we accept the thesis that crises are part of everyday ordinary life, and that one purpose of religion is to lessen the stress from myriad changes encountered, then one approach to religious education should be to take advantage of the "teachable moments" that a crisis presents. A "teachable moment" occurs when a person's defense mechanism is weakened and his ego is more open to outside influences and change—when a person feels out of control, discombobulated, and seeks to regain equilibrium. In "Crisis Theory," Naomi Golan states,

> During the crisis situation . . . a minimal force can produce a maximal effect: a small amount of focused help appropriately given

> at the right time may be more effective than more extensive help when the person is less open to change [9, pp. 421-422].

Thus, a rabbi or educator who is present, caring, and a sensitive guide at the right time can have a more powerful impact than years of counseling.

Successful crisis resolution promotes ego growth by increasing the repertoire of possible responses to the crisis and thus becoming the opportunity for growth and change. One objective, then, of religious education ought to be to teach students how to use their religious community and traditions to deal with the life's trials. Educators must take advantage of the "teachable moments" that are sure to occur sometime during the course of a child's years in the religious school and use them as an opportunity for growth, change, and the investigation of a whole new set of different behaviors.

PREPARATION FOR THE INTRODUCTION OF A CRISIS-SENSITIVE CURRICULUM

1. The Crisis Team: Proactive Not Reactive

In preparing to use the crisis-sensitive curriculum as part of Jewish education, the concept must be included in the mission statement and philosophy of the school. Next, the school must establish a "Crisis Team" comprised of a cross-section of congregants (particularly those working professionally in social work and child and adolescent psychology), the Educational Director, Family Education Coordinator, Youth Advisors, "crisis" teachers, parents, Rabbi, and members of the congregation with a deep understanding of Jewish sources.

The Team will meet on a regular basis to design a spiralling crisis curriculum and prepare a theoretical plan to handle various crises, that is, death of a student or teacher, a community incident, natural disaster, crisis in Israel, etc. The Team would be on-call so that should a major crisis occur, it would immediately convene to determine the optimal means of handling the situation and their role in helping; it would also be available to give suggestions, support, and assistance to classroom teachers. The Team would train teachers to familiarize themselves with Jewish sources, and use "anticipatory guidance, rehearsal for reality, and learning of new social and interpersonal skills" [9, p. 439]. Thus, the school would be proactive, always prepared for a crisis rather than scrambling to decide what to do when one does occur.

How a given crisis is handled will necessarily depend upon the nature of that crisis and the people involved. Some crises will necessitate the involvement of the entire school, such as the death of one of the students, teachers, or rabbi. Others might involve only a few students, as in the violation of school norms/rules. An integral part of the curriculum at every grade level, beginning in the middle school, will be one class focusing on crisis inter-vention. An occasional session for younger students on family changes, death of a pet or grandparent, serious illness, or divorce, could also be included in the curriculum. Concurrent parent discussion groups would apprise them of classroom activities and familiarize them with Jewish sources.

2. "Crisis" Teacher Background and Preparation

"Crisis" teachers will require special background. They will have to be good listeners, know how to lead students to explore choices, and have knowledge of Jewish sources. Teachers must be instructed to keep the class moving along an educational track and not allow it to develop into a "group therapy" session. In addition, teachers will also need to understand the role of guilt and guilt relieving techniques, especially the concept of "*T'shuva*" (asking for forgiveness and making amends, both with others and with God). Most importantly, the faculty will need to know how to instill hope into every situation and help the children develop faith. In this sense, faith or "faithing," (as defined by Dr. James Fowler) "is the process by which a person finds and makes meaning of life's significant questions and issues, adheres to this meaning, and acts it out in his/her life span" [10, p. 130]. Ultimately, teachers will be dealing with various coping skills gleaned from the psychology of Jewish tradition.

3. Class Recruitment

Theoretically, this class will be a regular part of the curriculum. If this is not possible, it could be an elective for which students would either volunteer or are persuaded by their teachers to do so. In any case, participants must understand that this class is a community which will look at the difficulties of growing up and then work together to find acceptable solutions. Ideally, at the beginning of the year, a weekend retreat would be held to help the students get to know each other better, build trust, and involve them in creating the classroom rules such as: no laughing at another's problems, no sharing of stories outside the classroom, etc. Writes John Dewey in *Experience in Education*,

> There is, I think, no point in the philosophy of progressive education which is sounder than its emphasis upon the importance of the participation of the learner in the formation of the purposes which direct his activities in the learning process, just as there is no defect in traditional education greater than its failure to secure the active co-operation of the pupil in construction of the purposes involved in his studying [8, p. 67].

Even if a full weekend retreat were not possible, students should be encouraged to "establish the rules," develop a structure, and get to know each other in an extra-classroom program.

4. Four Categories of Crisis

The very nature of a crisis as "a disruption of the equilibrium of daily living" makes it difficult to categorize these events. On the other hand, most crises will probably fall into one of the following four categories:

A. Immediate crises presented by life.
B. Serious violations of community norms.
C. Future crises students will have to face.
D. Remote crises that do not touch the students' lives directly, but trigger their concern for humanity.

Let us now examine each of these areas and suggest methods for assisting students to cope with each type of crisis.

A. Immediate Crisis Presented by Life

> We are assembled with our friends in the shadow that has fallen on their home. We raise our voices together in prayer to the Source of life, asking for comfort and strength. We need light when gloom darkens our home; to whom shall we look, but the Creator of light? We need fortitude and courage when pain and loss assail us; where shall we find them if not in the thought of Him who preserved all that is good from destruction? [1, p. 645].

In this category fall the major life traumas such as death, divorce, or sexual or physical abuse, as well as life changes such as moving, or simply encountering a new disruptive experience—any event that affects a single individual. Other more remote events, such as the death of a national leader, a national trauma (e.g. the explosion of the Challenger Shuttle), the outbreak of the Gulf War, threats to Israel, etc., affect every student in the school. Too often the school curriculum does not allow time to grapple with these issues, nor are there specific plans formulated to manage these situations. To let any of these crises go by without acknowledging and confronting them would be a major *faux pas* for religious education. We will use death as our example here.

Erich Lindemann states, religious agencies have led in dealing with the bereaved. They have provided comfort by giving the backing of dogma to the patient's wish for continued interaction with the deceased, have developed rituals that maintain the patient's interaction with others, and have counteracted the morbid guilt feelings of the patient by references to divine grace and by promising him an opportunity for "making up" to the deceased at the time of a later reunion [11, p. 18]. By dealing with death in a religious setting, teachers and students are able to derive comfort from rituals, prayers, and traditions. By practicing Jewish mourning customs followed by a discussion of their meanings, students will be better able to do what was intended by such observances: deal with the pain of bereavement. Students will be able to explore their feelings and express their sorrows, sense, of loss, and guilt feeling in a supportive community. In addition, students will be able to work through an acceptable formulation of their future relationship to the deceased and explore new patterns of conduct in the shadow of their loss. Students will learn that one is not alone in bereavement, and that through mourning customs and rituals Judaism provides community support through all stages of grief.

As an aside, a loss experienced need not be just for a human being. In a society where families are often separated by miles, pets play a significant role in the life of a family. The death of a pet should not be taken lightly. It can have a powerful impact and should be numbered among the many crises that young people will have to face. Also, other losses, for example, changes of relationships, people who move away, etc., need to be acknowledged and dealt with as seriously as a death.

When the death of a student, teacher, or major congregational figure occurs, the best way to handle the situation would be for the Crisis Team to first meet with the teachers to assess their feelings and provide suggestions for dealing with students' reactions. Afterward, the teachers and the Team would hold small group sessions in the Religious School, encouraging and giving time for students to ventilate their emotions. Lastly, a memorial service might be appropriate, with an emphasis upon the prayers and traditions which help one make sense of a tragedy. As an aside, should a suicide occur within the school community, the school should follow the above with particular concentration on avoiding martyrdom of the deceased.

Since guilt is always a predominant emotion after a loss, it would be important in class to talk about guilt feelings and how one relieves them. This is an optimal time to discuss "reality" versus "wishful thinking," that is, to talk about one's perceived role in causing another person's death and the reality of what one could actually have done to prevent it.

As religious tradition gives people a way to keep the memory of the deceased alive, this would be an essential area to explore with students. Perhaps the establishment of some type of memorial, gift to the congregation, or action program done in the person's memory would be appropriate at this time in order to teach students customary and apt ways to memorialize the deceased. Lastly, it is important to remember that dealing with the crisis of death is not a one-time event. Over and over it will be necessary to revisit the crisis, especially on significant occasions which highlight the absence of the deceased.

B. Serious Violation of the Norms of the Community

> . . . and of every herb You made, and every beast, You said that they were good; but when You made us in Your image, You did not say of us in Your Torah that humanity was good. Why, Lord? And God answered. . . Because you I have not yet perfected, because through the Torah you are to perfect yourselves, and to perfect the world. All other things are completed; they cannot grow. But humankind is not complete; you have yet to grow. Then I will call you good [1, p. 185].

Although we worry about how we, as educators, will handle the crisis of a death in the congregation, these events are, thank God, few and far between. On the other hand, the entire school faces continuing critical situations when they must deal with the inappropriate behavior of students. Such behavior includes abusive language, swearing, constant "put-downs," sexual innuendos, bullying, hitting, or controlling the classroom discussion by acting out. Any of the aforementioned can turn into an educator's worst nightmare, as handling the disruptive student is a problem that can overwhelm everyone involved in the school. Often, the single complaint of the "serious learner" is that they can not stand the behavior of others.

In one sense, dealing with disruptive students in the religious school is no different from dealing with them in a public school where teachers and principals experience such problems all the time. On the other hand, in a religious school, because of its small size and part-time nature, the disruption is magnified and thus the insolent student has a much greater impact. In addition, because of the voluntary nature of a religious school (families choose for their children to attend), and the ineffectiveness of penalties that work in other settings (e.g., poor grades in religious school will not effect chances of getting into college), discipline becomes more difficult. It is incumbent upon the religious school community to find an acceptable and effective way of controlling behavior. This can be accomplished by two methods: 1) holding up appropriate conduct rooted in our religious outlook, and 2) involving the students in self-governing.

1. Pursuing the "Good" It must be remembered that the basis of religion is the teaching of self-discipline. Be it the kinds of kosher foods one is permitted to eat, the reciting of a blessing before eating, the establishment of a fixed time for prayer, the observance of rest on Shabbat, Judaism teaches us discipline and the making of "*havdalah*"—the ability to distinguish between the sacred and the profane. This concept is then to be carried over into everyday life through conduct.

In one sense, leading a child to the self-discipline of rituals such as *kashrut* (laws dealing with kosher food) is simple. Keeping kosher is qualitative and can be judged; it has the immediate reward of feeling good that one did as God commanded. Keeping kosher is like being on a diet: one feels immediate gratification with each proper meal eaten. Soon, if the diet works, not only does the dieter feel good about himself, but comes to abhor and refrain from eating fattening foods. As we all know, the best diets are those leading to modification in eating patterns.

On the other hand, *Tikkun Ha-Middot* (the improvement of character) is a more difficult undertaking. In a religious school, improvement of character involves "trying on" good behaviors (e.g. to "imitate" God, to recognize that all are created in God's image and that we must act in a loving manner toward one another). It means that behavior patterns used in public school can be left at the door of the religious school and new behaviors can be "tested." It means holding up the idea of *kedusha* (holiness) before students and challenging them to achieve it. It means rewarding them for goodness instead of punishing the bad. Hopefully, such testing of behaviors and fulfilling of expectations will lead to changes in impulses, inclinations, passions, and desires. Modification of behavior is a priority in Jewish education. Since human beings lack the instinctual maps used by animals, religion helps us determine which choices to make. People seek guidance in deciding what type of person they want to be. Ideally, such ground-work in decision-making should be laid within the home and should be an ongoing process throughout childhood and the young adult years. However, too often parents try to abdicate this responsibility to institutions. We must return this responsibility to the families by working with them to not only recognize right and wrong, but then, being aware of both choices, decide in favor of right. Religion, in its proper form, does exactly that.

Louis Ginzberg, writing on the life of the great Rabbi Israel Salanter, tells us:

> The keynote of his [Rabbi Israel Salanter's] teaching is that the aim and task of the Jews is to strive to secure the ethically ideal condition of man and of the world, no matter how far off and perhaps unreachable it may be. Judaism is for him no theoretical system, teaching speculative truths of scientific knowledge concerning a certain province of thought, but it is a doctrine intended to lead man to his moral ennoblement by prescribed ways and means. . . If morality is to be not merely a theory but a real factor in the life of man, he must so train his thoughts and feelings that his moral consciousness becomes too strong to allow him to act otherwise than morally. The religious truths which are indispensable to the ethical education of man and without which he cannot develop morally, are: Belief in God, Revelation, and Reward and Punishment [12, pp. 178-179].

We draw near to the ethical ideal by always thinking of it and by examining everything in its light. This would be the objective of such a class on crisis education. Conducted in the safe environment of a community open to examining behaviors against the Jewish religious standard of conduct, students would subsequently reward each other for living according to the ideal. They would take moral conduct seriously, declare self-discipline as a virtue, and would become the "prophets" who would lead others to proper conduct.

2. Self-Governance If we, as leaders in religious schools, are to take behavioral crises seriously, we ought to learn from public schools which are currently training students in conflict resolution techniques and empowering them to take control of their lives by establishing student courts. Rabbi Jeffrey Schein suggests in, "What We Know About Moral Education,"

> Several educators have tried to address the issue of the "hidden curriculum" of Jewish schools. I have helped day schools in Los Angeles and Philadelphia initiate a *Beit Tzedek / Beit Din* [student court], an experiment in Jewish moral democracy involving students

> in making decisions about justice and fairness from Jewish/moral perspectives. It assumes that since fairness pertains to issues that emerge on the playground and in the classroom. In essence, an attempt can be made to make the social and moral issues that students live between classes an important part of a Jewish school's work in moral education. The implicit message of this program is that we care about the Jewish values students demonstrate as well as the ones they study. *Batei din* now function in a dozen Solomon Schechter schools throughout the country [13, p. 257].

Addressing the violation of the norms of a religious school needs to be considered as part of the very essence of a religious school. Recognition that such problems are bound to occur offers a wonderful opportunity for students to involve themselves in moral education and participate in an on-going examination of their own behavior. Just imagine the lessons that students who serve on the court will learn: leadership and decision-making skills, an understanding of the need for rules, fairness, compassion, and a familiarity with Jewish sources to guide them in deciding on verdicts. Although they would not be required to follow *Halacha* (Jewish law), if they chose not to do so, they would have to explain why. Also, one might imagine that other students, to avoid coming before the *Beit Tzedek*, would find means to settle disputes and police one another.

C. Future Crises

> How much we need You, O God, in days of trial! We need faith to live, faith in Your creative power that overcomes chaos and stirs all life toward a new and better world. We seek You, O God: thereby we grow in vision, as we elevate our souls beyond the sordid to the sacred.
>
> Your presence is the light piercing the darkness on our way, lighting our steps, making us see beauty and worth in all human beings [1, p. 185].

If crisis means any change that a person confronts which disturbs the equilibrium of living, be it health, security or the changing of relationships, then there is not a student in our religious school who will not be touched by a crisis during these important developmental years. The greatest service we as educators can do for our students is not to shield them from crises, but rather teach them how to cope with, learn from, and find meaning from them. The greatest gifts are the skills to weigh alternatives, understand choices, and consider possible solutions. What better way to lessen anxiety than to prepare to handle the possible pitfalls that could occur from a particular choice? What better way to lessen anxiety than to teach the rituals and traditions which allow them to ultimately identify with something much larger, more powerful, and more permanent than themselves? To accomplish the above goals, educators must first understand the psychological and personal conflicts young people experience at different stages of maturation, then identify the appropriate Jewish stories, laws, rituals, traditions, prayer, actions, etc., that address these issues.

What are some of those concerns? In a study conducted with Tucson's Jewish youth, Marilyn Haas and Betty Newlon found students ranked the following issues as most important:

41.0 percent — looks and appearance
40.8 percent — getting along with siblings
37.7 percent — hard to know whom to trust
35.1 percent — college and career choice
34.6 percent — hard to talk about feelings
32.2 percent — boredom
31.1 percent — getting along with friends

"Looks and appearance" ranked highest for junior high students and third for high school students. "Getting along with parents and friends" and "loneliness," although not in the top 10 percent, ranked in the upper percentile for all students [14, p. 44-45].

Since as educators, we can predict that young people will face these traumas, we must design a curriculum that addresses them as a community. For instance, we know that sixth graders will face the daily changing of friendships. One day, a child is in the "in group," and the next day, "out." Although we know that sixth graders are frequently mean to one another, we need to sensitize them that this is not appropriate behavior, and that others are hurt by their words. We can help them explore the meaning of friendship and the values they might have to compromise to join the "in group."

We know that junior high school students will deal with the issues of popularity, their growing sexuality, and their often conflicting emotions. High school students will have to decide how they will conduct themselves sexually, how to deal with peer pressure regarding drugs, cheating, etc. Both age groups will have to decide what happiness means to them and what makes them feel good about themselves. In addition, we must prepare them to handle grief or loss situations, be it the break-up of boyfriend/girlfriend relationship (often the source of depression leading to suicide), leaving home for college, or the actual death of a fellow student, pet, or family member.

As most young people at this age are relatively untouched by death, this would be a perfect time to explain mourning customs and rituals. A good idea for high school students would be a field trip to a funeral home. For many this will be their first visit. What better way to be exposed to the difficult task of preparing for the funeral of a loved one than when one is totally unemotional and all the magic and superstition can be debunked. (Every year for the past 20 years, I have taken 10th graders to visit a funeral home, and I can testify that these former students were better prepared to handle a loss in later years than were older members of the family who had never been exposed to such an experience.) This is also the time to teach about the *vidui* (death confessional) as well as various concepts of life after death and delineate how such concepts bring hope to the living and to the dying.

Judaism addresses all of the above-mentioned through rituals, prayers, stories, and traditions. *Mitzvot* (commandments), acts of *g'milut hasadim* (good deeds), and the giving of *tzedakah* (charity) help change moments of depression and guilt into a time of healing. Interestingly, the concept of Shabbat actually teaches people how to handle crises, for we are taught to pause on Shabbat, to pull back, reflect, take a breather, then return to the situation with new hope.

In classes on Crisis Education, Jewish values such as *Pikuach Nefesh* (the saving of a human life), *Kevod Atzmo* (self-respect), and *B'Tzelem Elohim* (in the image of God) can be emphasized as means of deciding what values are most important in life. Through the use of *aggadah* (folklore) and *midrash* (rabbinic sermons), many dilemmas can be brought to life so that students can learn how others deal with them. C. Moran states, "One of the marks of a community is the story its people hold in common, a story expressed in symbols, codes of behavior, styles of humor, modes of dress and address, ways of sharing sorrow and the like" [15, p. 131]. Stories ultimately offer "both a model for understanding the world and a guide for acting in it" [16, p. 131]. By selecting appropriate story material, the very youngest religious school student can benefit from this approach. Writes Peninna Schram in an article in the *Jewish Book Annual:*

> A story is an effective way to teach religion, traditions, values and customs, a creative way to introduce characters and places and an imaginative way to instill hope. Stories teach us how to live and, above all, show us what legacies to transmit to our future generations [17, p. 73].

In addition, crisis classes can teach compassion and concern by accepting the responsibility of caring for others in the community, enabling one to gain insight on preparing oneself for a similar crisis. For instance, one class could be responsible for enhancing joyous celebrations in the congregation by sending cards to the family celebrating the event, or doing something in the religious school for their fellow student whose family is celebrating a special occasion such as the birth of a brother or sister, or the marriage of a divorced parent. Another grade level could send condolence cards to those who have had a loss, or they could make a bereavement visit to the student's home. A discussion of the "upheavals" and difficulties of preparation for the Bar/Bat Mitzvah celebration could be held in the sixth grade year. Families who have recently had a ceremony could share their experiences which include the family squabbles and difficulties in decision-making. Congregants will gain comfort from learning that they are not the only family experiencing traumas in the midst of their joy. Ultimately, religious schools have a unique opportunity to offer ideas, suggestions of appropriate behavior and choices as to how to handle the future crises which young people are bound to face.

D. Remote Crises that Indirectly Touch Students' Lives

> Eternal God, we face the morrow with hope made stronger by the vision of Your kingdom, a world where poverty and war are banished, where injustice and hate are gone. Teach us more and more to share the pain of others, to heed Your call for justice, to pursue the blessing of peace. Help us, O God, to gain victory over evil, to bring nearer the day when all the world shall be one [1, p. 620].

Television and global communication expose young people to crises taking place halfway around the world. The bombing of Iraq takes place in their living rooms as well as on the desert sands. International reports of anti-Semitism bring to life the often precarious situation of Jews in society. Starving children in Somalia are real and not just a nebulous idea imposed by Mom and Dad when chiding their children to eat everything on their plates. The homeless and downtrodden are no longer invisible, but are viewed nightly on the news and special reports. In the Tucson, Arizona study mentioned above, students listed the three global issues of "homeless and hunger," "Soviet Jewry," and "nuclear destruction" among their top ten concerns. "Environmental pollution" was included within the top twenty. (This is a 3-year-old study; today, it is likely that "environmental concerns" would be higher on the list and "Soviet Jewry" would be eliminated as a concern.)

Most students today are not one-dimensional vapid human beings worried only about themselves, but are concerned about the world which they will inherit tomorrow. High on their agenda would be learning how they can participate in *Tikun Olam* (the repair of the world). Our Jewish tradition has much to say about the ideal world, with discussion about the poor, the environment, care of animals, the aged, and the sick. These Jewish values, which are often taught as social action concepts, need to be expressed in this curriculum as solutions to "crises" that, although remote, do effect students' lives. A "*Tikun Olam* Committee" could be formed in the classroom to study issues, write to legislators, and meet with community leaders. They could also help organize others in the school to participate in community projects such as cleaning up a neighborhood, repairing a dilapidated home, or serving hot meals to the hungry.

Students would soon realize that religious school is not just a place where people learn history and Hebrew, but a community that cares about others and deals with issues which affect the future. These types of activities will ultimately endow students with community-oriented values and the knowledge that they can make a difference in the world. At a time when many seem to be turning away from organized religion, these activities provide an opportunity to put religious ideals and faith into practice, and can ultimately help give direction and meaning to young people.

ADVANTAGES AND DISADVANTAGES OF A CRISIS-SENSITIVE CURRICULUM

A religious school educator reading this chapter will recognize that schools are already involved in many of the activities listed above. Thus, what makes this curriculum different from what is currently available? The answer is the *mindset* with which the administrator and teacher approach their teaching assignments. Instead of AIDS, war, and euthanasia simply being topics of theoretical discussion, they become real issues of daily life. No longer is the school reactive to problems and issues, but it is proactive, always prepared to handle situations. With a crisis-sensitive curriculum in place, we will send the message that the issues and concerns which cause anxiety in the students are viewed seriously by educators, and that we are here to support them with friendship, concern, and the resources from religious traditions.

A crisis-sensitive curriculum offers students classes in which they are free to discuss problems and explore alternatives. Teachers are more sensitive because they have been trained to observe body language and respond to statements revealing troubling concerns. In fact, teachers are given permission not only to abandon the subject matter of the day in favor of dealing with individual crises, but are expected to do so. Although parts of the curriculum are geared to anticipated crises, the curriculum is flexible enough to be amended with no real goals except to be a supportive community. Of course, one advantage is that prayers and blessings, rituals, and customs which were taught previously in other courses now become integrated into a course of study and subsequently take on new meanings. Built into the system would be opportunities to create new traditions and develop creative prayers which could strengthen students' abilities to cope with anxiety. Perhaps through prayer and community support, students might realize that much of the suffering they experience is not a result of the actual event, but instead how one relates to it.

A crisis-sensitive curriculum also has the advantage of forging a relationship between the synagogue and local mental health organizations, such as the Jewish Family Service Association. Human service organizations can lead training workshops for teachers, staff, and parents, lead student workshops on "normal adolescence," sexuality, suicide, etc., and can be used as referral agencies for individually counseling. In the final analysis, such a curriculum will not only lead a student to grow in knowledge, but develop as a *mensch* (human being) and become more mature.

Of course, a crisis-sensitive curriculum does contain some disadvantages. It may be difficult to find teachers with the skills and training to deal with such crises as well as the background to integrate Jewish tradition into the subject matter. It may also be hard to find teachers who are willing to dedicate what could be many hours of extra-classroom follow-up. The curriculum calls for highly skilled teachers who are flexible enough to readily change directions, yet prepared with materials for the continuity of the planned curriculum. Teachers, of course, will need to identify outside resource people who can help with both the emotional and psychological aspects of problem solving as well as the Judaic content. Teachers must also be able to acknowledge when a problem warrants outside intervention by either the Crisis Team or a private counselor.

SUMMARY

How does a young person gain self-understanding, self-control, and self-direction in a world with so many alternatives? Should these questions seem remote, then consider the words of a student speaker at a recent Stanford University graduation, who described his classmates as "not knowing how it relates to the past or the future, having little sense of the present, no life-sustaining beliefs, secular or religious, and consequently no goals and no path of effective action" [18, p. 25].

When one's secular belief system fails, where can one turn for help? Secularist Daniel Bell suggests, "an unfashionable answer—the return of Western society to some conception of religion. . . . What religion can restore is the continuity of generations, returning us to the existential predicaments which are the ground of humility and care for others" [19, p. 15].

> Rabbi Samuel Dresner continues this thought:For the truth is that religion is not simply magic or illusion. It speaks to the human condition. Religion provides "a set of coherent answers to the core existential questions"—birth, death, success, failure, illness, health, temptation, happiness—codifies its answers in a creed which has meaning for those who believe in it; celebrates them in rites which provide an emotional bond for those who participate; and establishes congregations for those who share this creed and celebration [19, p. 15].

Congregational religious schools have a unique opportunity and responsibility to use methods different from those available in public school classrooms. Religious educators can appeal to text, traditions, prayers, and rituals, and have the ability to find hope in every upheaval of life, from dealing with the smallest disappointment to the darkest hours of a student's life. Religious educators can give students a sense of faith in every occasion even when the forces of the world seem to be conspiring against them, and they can help students find meaning even in the midst of despair.

REFERENCES

1. *Gates of Prayer: The New Union Prayer Book,* Central Conference American Rabbis, New York, 1975.
2. G. Caplan cited by Lydia Rappaport, The State of Crisis: Some Theoretical Considerations, in *Crisis Intervention: Selected Readings,* H. J. Parad (ed.), Family Services Association of America, New York, 1965.
3. G. Caplan cited by N. Golan, Crisis Theory, in *Social Work Treatment: Interlocking Theoretical Approaches,* F. J. Turner (ed.), The Free Press, New York, 1974.
4. R. Schmidt, *Exploring Religion,* (2nd Edition), Wadsworth, Belmont, California, 1990.

5. D. Coleman, Family Rituals May Promote Better Emotional Adjustment, *New York Times,* March 11, 1992, reprinted in *Working With Interfaith Couples: A Jewish Perspective,* United American Hebrew Congregations, New York, 1992.
6. G. Sheehy, *Pathfinders,* William Morrow, New York, 1981.
7. Z. Yehuda, *The Role of Prayer in School: A Circular Outlook*, unpublished paper, 1972.
8. J. Dewey, *Experience and Education,* Collier Books, New York, 1938.
9. N. Golan, Crisis Theory, in *Social Work Treatment: Interlocking Theoretical Approaches,* F. J. Turner (ed.), The Free Press, New York, 1974.
10. J. W. Fowler, *Stages of Faith,* Harper & Row, San Francisco, California, 1981, cited by Roberta Louis Goodman, What We Know About . . . Faith Development, in *What We Know About Religious Education,* S. L. Kelman (ed.), Torah Aura Productions, Los Angeles, California, 1992.
11. E. Lindemann, Theoretical Explorations, in *Crisis Intervention: Selected Readings,* H. J. Parad (ed.), Family Service Association of America, New York, 1965.
12. L. Ginzberg, *Students, Scholars and Saints,* Jewish Publication Society, Philadelphia, Pennsylvania, 1928.
13. J. Schein, What We Know About Moral Education, in *What We Know About Jewish Education,* S. L. Kelman (ed.), Torah Aura Productions, Los Angeles, California, 1992.
14. M. Haas and B. Newlon, Voices From the Desert: Concerns of Tucson's Jewish Youth, *Journal of Jewish Communal Service, 67*:1, Fall 1990.
15. C. Moran, *Religious Education Development: Images For the Future,* Winston Press, Minneapolis, Minnesota, 1983, cited by Roberta Louis Goodman, What We Know About . . . Faith Development, in *What We Know About Religious Education,* S. L. Kelman (ed.), Torah Aura Productions, Los Angeles, California, 1992.
16. M. Goldberg, *Jews and Christians: Getting Our Stories Straight: The Exodus and Passion-Ressurection,* Abingdon Press, Nashville, Tennesee, cited by Roberta Louis Goodman, What We Know About . . . Faith Development, in *What We Know About Religious Education,* S. L. Kelman (ed.), Torah Aura Productions, Los Angeles, California, 1992.
17. P. Schram, Current Collection of Jewish Folktales, in *Jewish Book Annual, 49,* 1991-92.
18. W. V. Wishard, The American Future: A Perspective for Education, delivered at the Center for Educational Leadership, Lansing, Michigan, June 19, 1992, cited in *Vital Speeches of the Day,* October 15, 1992.
19. S.H. Dresner, Modernity Exhausted, *Jewish Spectator, 57*:1, Spring 1992.

CHAPTER 6

The Crisis of Youth Suicide

Diane Ryerson and John Kalafat

Adolescent suicides have a devastating impact on schools, families, and communities. When a student dies by his own hand, educators are compelled to both manage the school systems shock and grief while, at the same time, to attempt to identify and intervene with other teens who might make similar self destructive decisions. This chapter encourages both educators and parents to take a *proactive* approach to the tragedy of youth suicide.

SCOPE OF THE PROBLEM

Current facts about adolescent suicidal behavior provide a compelling rationale for schools and communities to be prepared, in advance, to respond to such behavior.

- Suicide completions rank as the third leading cause of death among adolescents (behind accidents and homicide). The current rates are probably underestimates, as many accidents and some homicides may actually be suicides. While adequate data is scarce, school and mental health personnel have begun to report increased suicidal behavior in pre-teens.
- The current adolescent suicide rate in the United States is approximately twelve per 100,000 (17 per 100,000 for white males). Males complete suicide about four times more often than females, possibly because they are more prone to use more lethal means (the most common method is guns) [1].
- It is estimated that there may be up to 100 attempts for every completion. In a variety of surveys throughout the country, about

10 percent of adolescents indicate that they have made a suicide attempt; females attempt suicide about eight times more often than males [2].

- Suicide attempts can result in serious injury, and youth who have made suicide attempts are significantly more likely than the general adolescent population to ultimately kill themselves.
- Suicidal thoughts and even attempts are more likely to be known to a teenagers peers than to adults. Surveys indicate that about one-half of the female respondents and between one-fourth and one-third of the male respondents report knowing a teen who has seriously talked about or attempted suicide. All teens have been exposed to media, music, literature and performing arts depicting or reporting suicide attempts and completions [3].
- It is estimated that only one-fourth of teens who know of a suicidal peer report this to an adult, partly due to the importance of maintaining a confidence, and partly due to their concerns about adults' responses [3].

While these figures indicate that schools and communities can correctly assume that a suicide completion is an infrequent event, they clearly show that all school personnel must be prepared to deal with at-risk youth, suicide attempts, and students returning to school after an attempt. In addition, teenagers who encounter these phenomena among their peers (and, in our experience, occasionally among school personnel and other adults in the community), need to know how to identify suicidal warning signs and obtain professional help.

THE SCHOOL'S RESPONSIBILITY

Overburdened school personnel may rightly ask how they should respond to such self destructive behavior. The short answer is that their role is both *crucial* and *limited,* and they must carry out this role as part of a total community effort. The school's responsibilities fall in three areas:

1. *Identification:* Schools are the sole compulsory institution serving youth in this country and, therefore, have access to them in a relatively structured environment for more of their waking hours than parents or other adults in the community. Behavioral changes in students that indicate they are experiencing self-destructive thoughts and impulses are often more easily detected in the school setting. Such changes may include drops in performance, atypical (for that student) misbehavior, withdrawal, fatigue, or negative themes in written materials.

2. *Support and response:* A federal statute (PL 94-142) and many similar state statutes mandate a role for public school in addressing a broad range of student problems, including the impact of emotional difficulties on academic performance [4]. Also, most states have a statue similar to California's Code of Ethics of the Teaching Profession (Section 80130 of the California Administrative Code, Title 5), Principle 1 of which refers to protecting the health and safety of students [5]. Because of these broad protective mandates, schools hire a variety of trained personnel such as nurses, counselors, and mental health consultants. Moreover, teachers and other staff often have personal contacts with students, particularly outside of class. These mandates empower educators to reach out to troubled students, as well as be approached by students for help.

Although some schools may be equipped to provide psychological counseling, school personnel need not be *required* to provide these services since it could tax limited school resources. A supportive initial response and a personally made referral for additional help is all that is required. Policies and procedures should be developed to guide school staff in the identification and referral of at-risk students. In addition, referral and consultative agreements should be established proactively with key community care givers including emergency, law enforcement and mental health personnel.

3. *Education:* This is, of course, the primary mandate of the school. Faculty, staff, and parents must learn how to identify and respond to troubled students, as well as become familiar with community resources and the procedures for accessing them. A broad range of school personnel have acknowledged this role and have expressed a need for additional training in identification, crisis response and referrals [4, 6, 7].

PROGRAM COMPONENTS

Comprehensive programs which address the crisis of youth suicide are referred to as suicide *prevention* programs since this it the primary goal of such endeavors. The goals of comprehensive school based suicide prevention programs are threefold:

1. *Prevention:* To prevent the occurrence of self-destructive behavior and completed suicides in school communities.
2. *Intervention:* To intervene swiftly, appropriately and in a supportive manner when students are at-risk for self-destructive behavior.

3. *Postvention:* To provide a supportive, healing environment in the following situations:
   a. When an individual student returns to school following a serious attempt, gesture and/or hospitalization.
   b. When the school community must cope with the aftermath of a suicide completion(s) or highly visible attempt(s).

Most comprehensive school based suicide prevention program emphasize educating the entire school community—educators and support staff, parents, and students themselves. These individuals are taught how to:

1. Identify an adolescent who is demonstrating warning signs.
2. Refer a troubled teen to an appropriate adult.

The focus of these programs is to enable all members of the school community to recognize a troubled teen and to provide them with step by step procedures for intervening in a suicidal crisis. By openly addressing a difficult, and often taboo, subject directly, these programs enhance the development and maintenance of a supportive, caring school climate. Because schools are the only institution that provides easy access to the majority of preadolescents and adolescents in our society, they are critical to suicide prevention efforts. In addition they also provide access to the adults who are closest to adolescents and most concerned with their welfare: teachers and parents.

Extensive experience has demonstrated that all members of an educational community play an important role in suicide prevention planning and, therefore, need explicit training appropriate to their role:

- *Administrators and Board of Trustees*: Need to recognize the severity of the problem and support the development and implementation of prevention, intervention and postvention activities.
- *Classroom teachers*: Need explicit training in how to recognize warning signs of potentially self destructive behavior in a classroom setting. They also need to master appropriate procedures for both interviewing and referring an at-risk child. They need the assurance that the school administration, Board of Trustees and peers will support their efforts.
- *Special student services staff*: Nurses, school social workers and psychologists, guidance counselors, drug abuse counselors are often called on to intervene with a suicidal student that has been identified by a teacher or classmate. They need specialized training on how to manage a self destructive teen.

- *Support staff*: Maintenance workers, cafeteria workers, bus drivers, secretaries, coaches, etc. see students in a less formal context than the classroom when students are less on their guard. They are often in a position to observe warning signs and identify the appropriate care givers.
- *Parents*: Have the most to lose, but are often the last to know when their child is at-risk because they may not recognize the severity of the problem. Often, the thought of their child being suicidal is so upsetting that their desire to deny the threat overcomes their ability to take appropriate action.
- *Students*: Clinical experience and research findings demonstrate that *students know first* when a friend is at-risk. Much of the time, teenagers directly or indirectly alert their peers when they are self destructive, while those at-risk teens may conceal their feelings from their parents and teachers. This is because adolescents routinely turn first to adolescents for understanding and assistance with their problems.

If teenagers do not know what to do or how to act when a friend confides s/he is suicidal or demonstrates warning signs, they may miss the opportunity to save a life. Since teens are the "rescuers of choice" of fellow teens, they need to know how to respond effectively. If not, they can be *overwhelmed*, afraid of embarrassing themselves or their friend, or they may *overreact*:

- They may be angry at the friend for placing them in a difficult situation.
- They may be resistant to tell anyone because they have been sworn to secrecy.
- They may not know what to say or they may joke around or minimize the problem, or
- They may not know when, how and where to get appropriate adult assistance [8].

While schools have used a variety of strategies to educate their communities, a comprehensive and cost effective approach to training the entire school community is a series of special tailored workshops for each group. The authors believe it is important to educate the responsible adults in the school community prior to introducing student curriculum. This is to allow parents, teachers, and staff to become comfortable with and knowledgeable about the subject *before* students are trained to turn to them for help when either they or a peer are troubled.

PREVENTION TRAINING

The training of an entire school community can be easily accomplished over an academic year. The following is a brief outline of the necessary sequential steps.

1. Administrator orientation: The superintendent, assistant superintendents, high school building principals and their assistants, directors of key areas such as guidance, special services, discipline, etc. participate in several educational/planning sessions with the external or internal trainers. The trainers are usually from a local mental health service provider or are a school employee at the director's level who has had specialized training in suicide prevention.

Goals are to:

- Educate administrators about the scope of the problem and possible prevention procedures.
- Decide on the content and format of training program selected.
- Appoint an internal school training team to undertake coordination of on-going training.
- Develop training schedule and resource allocation procedures.

2. For feedback and endorsement: Although some schools elect to bypass this step, it is often critical in the acceptance and eventual institutionalization of prevention programs.

3. Internal Team Training: This team is selected by administration to coordinate and deliver the training sessions to teachers, parents and students. The team is typically comprised of guidance counselors, school psychologists, social workers, nurses, health teachers, and substance abuse counselors. They are trained by either internal or external consultants. Team training should include:

- Details of training schedule outline.
- Modifications made to tailor selected program to needs of an individual school. There are some specific points which must be considered. These include:
  - a. History of recent attempts or completions;
  - b. School's current policy and procedures regarding self destructive students;
  - c. Linkage with local service providers; and
  - d. Schools demographics—gender, racial, ethnic, religious, and socioeconomic considerations.

4. Educators and support staff training: All teachers, administrators, professional support staff, and building support staff (or group

representatives) participate in a three to four hour educational seminar. This can be done at one time with the entire faculty or broken into two or three separate training sessions. It is important that the *entire* adult staff receive this training *before* parents or students become involved. This education is often accomplished during half day in-service training sessions.

5. Parents: It is often difficult to reach parents with this vitally important information because of their traditionally poor attendance at school-based functions, together with their understandable reluctance to address this issue directly. The participation of educators and students can be mandated; the involvement of parents is voluntary. Schools should consider a wide range of approaches to disseminating the information to parents including:

- PTO sponsored evening meetings
- Daytime meetings
- Presentation at housing developments, local service clubs and local houses of worship
- Print and electronic media education campaigns
- Mailed pamphlet with cover letter from the superintendent or principal.

6. Students: Students can receive this vital information through a specialized workshop (internal field trip) or within a health curriculum unit. A minimum of six hours should be devoted to the subject to insure adequate time to cover the salient points. Most schools target the incoming ninth or tenth grade, and repeat the program annually with the incoming class. Experience demonstrates that while background information can be presented in a large group, it is critical that students have the opportunity to discuss the issue and practice interventions in a small group setting. This can be accomplished in a classroom setting or small breakout group.

It is imperative that students learn this sensitive material from trainers who are comfortable with and knowledgeable about the subject. The small group discussion becomes an opportunity for students to evaluate the potential helpfulness and understanding of school employees *before* they are confronted with a suicidal crisis.

It is important that each of these participant groups learn the same basic information regarding identifying and helping teens at-risk. This will insure that everyone involved in a crisis is operating from the same basis of information and, hopefully, has the same attitudes and values toward intervening in a potential suicide. When only part of the faculty or student body has received this information, tragic misunderstandings can hamper effective intervention efforts.

RATIONALE FOR TRAINING STUDENTS IN SUICIDE PREVENTION

Because students are usually the first to know when a peer is at risk, educational programs that teach students how to respond to troubled teens and how to resist the pressure to maintain confidentiality and inform a responsible adult are crucial components of any prevention program. While hundreds of such student curricula exist [9], they remain a controversial component of school programs. This is due, in part, to a persistent *myth* that discussing suicide (like drugs, or sex) with adolescents will instigate such behavior. In addition, concern has been raised by the recent research indicating that media depicting, or vividly reporting, suicide completions, have been associated with increases in imitative behavior in certain troubled youths.

Myth

In regard to the myth, the previously cited surveys demonstrate that adolescents have already been exposed to suicidal behavior both in their peers and in the media. As Charlotte Ross, a pioneer in suicide school-based prevention has pointed out, it is better for students to learn appropriate responses to these phenomena in the classroom than in the street [10].

Imitation

In regard to the imitation issue, recent research indicates that when media presentations are accompanied by education, such as information about resources, coppycat attempts rarely occur. Imitation or "contagion" takes place when specific conditions, such as high emotional arousal, lack of information and inadequate intervention procedures exist. It is, therefore, prudent to exclude audio-visual materials that depict suicide attempts from school suicide prevention programs. These programs should emphasize constructive responses to troubled teens, help seeking behavior and locally available resources.

It should also be noted that student programs have been in existence for the past fifteen years. Many of these, including those developed by the authors, have been carefully tracked. *No evidence* exists that these programs have been associated with increased incidence of suicidal behavior (ADC, 1992). On the contrary, in several cases, the number of completed suicides in communities with such the number of completed suicides in communities with such programs in place have been found to be lower than in neighboring regions.

PREVENTION PROGRAM CONTENT

While existing models vary, the authors have found that most suicide awareness educational programs include the following essential elements. This basic information can be tailored to reflect the characteristics of the recipient group and the local community:

- Overview of a scope of the problem
- Identification of warning signs
- Brief review of assumed causes
    - biological
    - sociological
    - psychological
- How to assist a troubled teen
    - listening skills
    - problem solving
    - referral procedures
- Where and how to get adult and professional help, both within the school and in the larger community, twenty-four hours a day.

The aim of the prevention/education portion of school based programs is to alert school communities to the existence of at-risk students and to provide specific steps for managing a crisis. These programs are educational in nature. *They should not be confused with psychotherapy*. They are not designed to change longstanding negative attitudes in troubled youth, or to treat emotional or mental illness. They exist to give everyone in the school the basic knowledge and skills to deal with the reality of suicide.

UNDERSTANDING AND MANAGING RESISTANCE TO PREVENTION PROGRAMS

Occasionally, a school or sponsoring community agency will encounter resistance to the implementation of school based suicide prevention programming. It is essential that either the internal or external program director address each concern openly and thoroughly. Suicide, despite recent media attention, is still a frightening and repugnant issue that many people have difficulty discussing, especially with teenagers.

The authors' extensive experience has demonstrated that the initial resistance of schools fall into two overlapping categories:

1. Inaccuracies or misconceptions, and
2. Legitimate concerns regarding the program's content, process, time, and resource requirements.

The most common concern voiced by educator's and laymen alike is the fear that if you talk about suicide (or other high risk, controversial topics like drugs, homosexuality, aids and teen pregnancy and sexual behavior) with teens, you will plant the idea and precipitate their making an attempt. While there is no research or clinical data to support this fear, it is a tenacious concern that must be openly and frankly discussed.

Additional mistaken beliefs include:

- *Parents will be opposed to these programs*. Our experience shows parents welcome the schools initiative in addressing this difficult subject.
- *Legal consequences will follow if, after such a program, there is a subsequent suicide attempt by a student and the school is blamed.* All lawsuits, to date, involving school's culpability regarding an attempted or completed suicide have faulted schools for *not* having prevention programs in place.
- *There are no suicidal students in this school*. No school is immune. It's devastating to learn this the hard way.
- *It's better to let sleeping dogs lie.*
- *This type of program calls attention to suicide:* By addressing suicide in classroom, the program will convey to students that it is an acceptable way to deal with problems.

  Even the best adjusted preteens and teens are well aware of suicidal behavior because of its frequent portrayal in the news and entertainment media and because suicidal ideation and threats are all too common among their peers. Today's teen is, as well, often incorrectly informed about the realities of self-destructive behavior. Schools must decide whether they are willing to let them learn the facts on the street or from knowledgeable, caring adults.

On the other hand, many schools who are sincerely committed to the concept of suicide prevention become stymied by such realistic concerns as:

- Inadequate funding and/or personnel
- Overcrowded school calendar

- Overworked and/or resistant faculty
- Inadequate training/lack of expertise
- Lack of local resources for counseling or emergency referrals

Both categories of concerns can prevent a school from imitating this very important programming. Sufficient time should be allocated to addressing these resistances adequately *before* program is instituted.

Several strategies for addressing resistance include:

- Persistence
- Listen closely to administrators' concerns and tailor programs to meet the unique conditions of target districts, if appropriate.
- Minimize program's cost to the school by seeking foundation, state, or county funding.
- When possible, demonstrate the programs track record.
- Encourage administrators to consult with their professional colleagues at schools already participating in prevention programming.
- Provide sufficient training and consultation to insure that the school's internal project director is comfortable with the topic and materials and confident about referral procedures to local mental health providers.

INTERVENTION PROCEDURES

The management of both individual at-risk teens and specific suicidal crises is usually dictated by a school's written intervention procedures and programs. This is often the best developed section of a school's existing crisis programming. Important components include:

1. Broad board policy toward the recognition and management of self destructive behavior.
2. Specific procedures for dealing with various levels of suicidal behavior.
   - suicide threats
   - suicide gestures
   - suicide attempts
   - completed suicide (see postvention)

It is important that all faculty and support staff are aware of these procedures and that they are reviewed annually. Many schools include liaison agreements with local crisis and mental health service providers in their procedures.

When developing a policy, a school should first collect representative samples from similar districts, review their school's current explicit or implicit procedures, create a draft and request feedback from all key groups. Many schools include guidelines for managing a suicidal student's return to school following a threat or attempt. Experience and research concur that prior attempters are at heightened risk for repeated attempts and in need of well coordinated support.

Some schools provide a variety of support groups for vulnerable teens and/or facilitate their continuation with individual therapy either at school (via contract for service agreements with local mental health providers) or with local agencies and private practitioners.

POSTVENTION PROCEDURES

Postvention procedures address two situations: 1) Managing the aftermath of a completed suicide or nearly lethal attempt with the entire school community, and 2) ensuring a supportive school reentry for a student who had been hospitalized for a suicide attempt or serious threat. In the first situation, the goals are 1) to promote healing in the school community, and 2) to prevent inappropriate reactions including future suicide attempts. A standard process is now widely recommended and details are available elsewhere [11-13]. Briefly, the steps involved are:

1. Hold a meeting for faculty and staff prior to the next school day following the suicide in order to:
   - Allow faculty to share their reactions and receive support.
   - Develop a standard account to be provided to all students.
   - Initiate identification of other students who may be at risk for particularly strong reactions including suicidal behavior.
   - Inform staff of school's plans to deal with parents, the media, etc.
2. Prepare a statement to be read and discussed with students in their homeroom by classroom teachers or, if preferred, designated school officials. Announcement of the death should never be made over the public address system.
3. Establish drop-in support/crisis groups for students in convenient locations throughout the school—library, conference room, cafeteria, auditoriums, etc. Any student may be excused from class to attend. Support groups should be available for two to three days. Thereafter, troubled students can be dealt with individually.

4. Continue to meet with identified at-risk students on an as needed basis.
5. Schedule an open meeting for concerned parents as soon as possible, as they need to express their concerns, understand what the school is doing to cope with the tragedy and learn how to be supportive to their children. This meeting should be co-lead by the school principal and the medical health consultant.

   The media should *not* be invited to this meeting, but should be given a statement together with information regarding warning signs and referral services.
6. Conduct frequent debriefing with school officials (e.g., administration and crisis team) and hold a faculty meeting after several days.

   Additional considerations include:

   - One person, usually the principal, should be designated to talk with the media, and all inquiries should be directed to him/her. The school secretary should have a written statement to give or read to the press.
   - External consultants familiar with the school should lead or co-lead the postvention process, as the school staff are survivors themselves and all of the members of the school community (including administrators, teachers and staff members) need support and direction.
   - School should remain open and classes held during the aftermath; but academic requirements should be modified for up to a week. The goal is to provide a stable, supportive structured environment during the immediate postvention period.
   - Suicide education classes for students should be suspended for at least one semester; schools must be alert to postvention issues for at least a one-year cycle (through the anniversary) following the suicide.

Our experience indicates the provision of such structure and support following a completed or attempted suicide significantly reduces or eliminates subsequent attempts among the students and facilitates the school community's emotional healing. The cooperation and support of parents and community professionals (ensured through prior arrangements) is essential at this time. This joint effort can also help to avoid a situation which isolates and/or scapegoats the school.

The second aspect of postvention involves proactive coordination between local mental health providers and school personnel to ensure a supportive "holding environment" during a suicidal student's hospital discharge and school reentry. As Judie Smith, past cochairman of the

School Program Committee of the American Association of Suicidology, states in her 1991 paper on school reentry issues:

> Hospitalization is often recommended as a way of protection as well as providing necessary medical assistance for young people who have attempted suicide or in some instances made a serious suicide threat. By far the majority of teenagers who attempt suicide do not die from their desperate action. The period of time when the student first comes back to school following hospitalization is a particularly vulnerable time.
>
> A suicide attempt often conveys an ambivalence about living or dying. Very few young people have a determined desire to die. Their action is a dramatic way to communicate their overwhelming sense of helplessness and hopelessness. This message indicates a sense of powerlessness to change their life situation.
>
> School personnel are in a position to respond to their message of helplessness by facilitating a coordinated effort of the family, friends, therapist and school staff to help the young attempter regain a sense of control and relieve some of the sources of stress. An individualized re-entry plan for the student becomes an important part of crisis resolution [14].

Smith identified three major issues that require the school's attention when a student is returning to school together with possible strategies for addressing each issue.

ISSUE: *On-Going Support and Aftercare*
OPTIONS: Support group
Individual counseling session
Daily contact with counselor
Assign mentor
Nurse administer medication
Teachers monitor and give extra support
Request recommendations from hospital
Include volunteers or other students in support system
Refer to community aftercare group
Keep contact with therapist

ISSUE: *Transition from Hospital Setting*
OPTIONS: Establish relationship with hospital prior to release
Visit student in hospital
Attend discharge staffing
Hospital recommend academic changes
Reduce number and length of assignments
Offer make up work and/or tutorial help

ISSUE: *Behavior and Attendance Problems*
OPTIONS: Write behavior contract with student
Restructure rules
Request hospital recommendations
Teacher sensitive to unusual classroom behavior
Monitor attendance records

CONCLUSION

The dramatic increase in both adolescent suicide attempts and completions since the 1960s has forced schools to face this disturbing and tragic reality. As there are, to date, no universally accepted guidelines for managing this major public health problem, each school must take responsibility for proactive planning to address the continuum of problems posed by student self destructive behavior. Unfortunately, many schools wait until after a student has died at his or her own hand before they tackle the tough issue of suicide.

The impact of the completed suicide of a student or faculty member reaches far beyond the untimely death. The entire school community will be racked with waves of grief, remorse, guilt and shame which will not only disrupt the educational process, but also cause extreme emotional upheaval in many students and educators.

Proactive planning which provides prevention/awareness education for all members of the school community, the development of intervention strategies to direct the schools management of a suicidal threat or crisis and the creation of a step by step plan to manage the aftermath of a completed suicide will enable schools to address the reality of suicide *before* a tragedy occurs.

REFERENCES

1. National Center for Health Statistics, *Vital statistics of the United States; Vol. 2.* Mortality-Part A [for the years 1966-1988], U.S. Government Printing Office, Washington, D.C., 1968-1991.
2. K. Hawton, *Suicide and Attempted Suicide among Children and Adolescents,* Sage, Newbury Park, California, 1986.
3. J. Kalafat and M. Elias, Adolescents' Experience with and Response to Suicidal Peers, *Suicide and Life Threatening Behavior, 22,* pp. 315-321, 1992.
4. M. C. Grob, A. A. Klein, and S. V. Eisen, The Role of the High School Professional in Identifying and Managing Adolescent Suicidal Behavior, *Journal of Youth and Adolescence, 12,* pp. 163-173, 1982.
5. California State Department of Education, *Suicide Prevention Program for California Schools,* California State Department of Education, Sacramento, California, 1987.

6. J. Sandoval, Crisis Counseling: Conceptualizations and General Principles, *School Psychology Review, 14,* pp. 257-265, 1985.
7. P. S. Wise, V. S. Smead, and E. S. Huebner, Crisis Intervention: Involvement and Training Needs of School Psychology Personnel, *Journal of School Psychology, 25,* pp. 185-187, 1987.
8. D. Ryerson, Suicide Awareness Education in Schools: The Development of a Core Curriculum and Subsequent Modification for Special Populations or Institutions, *Death Studies, 14,* pp. 371-390, 1990.
9. K. Smith, J. Eyman, R. Dyck, and D. Ryerson, *Report of the School Suicide Programs Questionnaire,* Menninger Clinic, Albuquerque, New Mexico, 1987.
10. C. P. Ross, Teaching Children the Facts of Life and Death: Suicide Prevention in the Schools, in *Youth Suicide,* M. L. Peck, N. L. Farberow and R. E. Litman (eds.), Springer, New York, 1985.
11. American Association of Suicidology, *Suicide Prevention Guidelines: Suggestions for Dealing With the Aftermath of Suicide in the Schools,* American Association of Suicidology, Denver, 1990.
12. Centers for Disease Control, CDC Recommendations for a Community Plan for the Prevention and Containment of Suicide Clusters, *Morbidity and Mortality Weekly Report* (Supplement No. 5-6), *37,* pp. 1-12, 1988.
13. J. Kalafat and M. Underwood, *Lifelines: A School-based Adolescent Suicide Response Program,* Kendall/Hurt, Debuque, Iowa, 1989.
14. J. Smith, *Returning to School Following a Suicide Attempt,* paper presented at the Annual Conference of the American Association of Suicidology, April 1991.

BIBLIOGRAPHY

Caplan, G., *Principles of Preventive Psychiatry,* Basic Books, New York, 1964.

Centers for Disease Control, *Youth Suicide Prevention Programs: A Resource Guide,* Atlanta Centers for Disease Control, Atlanta, 1992.

Garland, A. F. and E. Zigler, Adolescent Suicide Prevention: Current Research and Social Policy Implications, *American Psychologist, 48,* pp. 169-182, 1993.

Hoff, L. A., *People in Crisis: Understanding and Helping,* Addison-Wesley, Redwood City, California, 1989.

Orbach, I., E. Rosenheim, and E. Hary, Some Aspects of Cognitive Functioning in Suicidal Children, *Journal of the American Academy of Child Adolescent Psychiatry, 26,* pp. 181-185, 1987.

Rotheram-Borus, M. L., P. D. Thrautman, S. C. Dopkins, and P. E. Shrout, Cognitive Style and Pleasant Activities among Female Adolescent Suicide Attempters, *Journal of Consulting and Clinical Psychology, 58,* pp. 554-561, 1990.

Ryerson, D., *School Based Suicide Prevention Programs: Identifying and Helping Troubled Teens,* paper presented at the Annual Suicide Conference Harvard Medical School, Boston, Massachusetts, January 1990.

Ryerson, D., ASAP—An Adolescent Suicide Awareness Program, in *Suicide in Adolescence,* R. F. W. Diekstra and K. Hawton (eds.), Martinus Nijhoff Publishers, The Netherlands, pp. 173-190, 1987.

CHAPTER 7

AIDS and HIV Infection: Today's Health Crises

Patricia Zalaznik

AIDS IS NOW THE SIXTH LEADING CAUSE OF DEATH FOR AGES 15-24 IN THE UNITED STATES [1].

"ONE OUT OF FIVE PEOPLE WHO HAS AIDS IS AGE 20 TO 30. THIS MEANS THEY WERE LIKELY TEENAGERS WHEN INFECTED" [2].

3,372 CHILDREN AGES 13 AND UNDER HAVE AIDS [2].

BY 1991, HIV WILL BECOME THE MAJOR INFECTIOUS CAUSE OF PEDIATRIC MENTAL RETARDATION IN THE UNITED STATES [3].

BETWEEN JANUARY 31, 1989 AND FEB. 1, 1990, THE NUMBER OF CASES AMONG 13-19 YEAR OLDS INCREASED BY 40% [4].

These are not screaming headlines from a sensational tabloid newspaper. They are recent reports from professional literature which alert us to the extraordinary and continuing challenges which HIV/AIDS presents to schools and communities.

The purpose of this chapter is to examine the need for and process of development of policies in school districts which will be called upon to serve students or staff infected with HIV virus or having AIDS. Careful and collaborative development of policies may educate all segments of the population and serve to prevent difficult situations occurring when it becomes known that an HIV infected individual is in the school setting. The chapter will also discuss related issues such as HIV education, death education, and counseling.

While the HIV/AIDS epidemic continues to increase, significant numbers of young people are still involved in risk-taking behaviors. This is indicated by rates of sexually transmitted disease (STD), pregnancy, and the frequency of sexual activity. STDs among adolescents are epidemic [5, 6]. According to the Guttmacher Institute "about 10 percent of teenage women get pregnant each year and 40 percent become pregnant before age 20" [7]. Sexual activity rates are estimated to be over 60 percent by twelfth grade [8, 9].

Legislation now requires inclusion of all types of students in schools and that their individual needs be met as appropriately as possible in the least restrictive environment. When the first individual in a school is identified as HIV positive, be it a young child, an adolescent, or a staff member, there is a new sense of urgency. An established district policy, accompanied by an action plan, is crucial to prevent a crisis. This situation will eventually occur in most schools, but, if the district is prepared, the situation need not become a crisis. Schools will be challenged to be proactive, compassionate, and creative. Being proactive may actually be a life-saving measure.

Commonly expressed feelings mentioned in association with HIV-infection include anger, fear, shame, denial, secrecy, guilt, anxiety, rage, inadequacy, isolation, vulnerability, grief, loneliness, hope, shock, despair, and depression. Reflecting upon these feelings and their impact on a school community presents a challenge. It may also sadden us. However, it is hoped that an understanding of the possible effects on the school community in the future they will motivate people to action *now*.

DEFINITIONS

"If policymakers understand these words, they will know why researchers urge that we talk about HIV, rather than simply discussing AIDS" [10]. "*HIV (Human Immunodeficiency Virus)* is the virus which causes a predictable, progressive impairment of the immune system (AIDS). Persons who are HIV infected may show no signs or symptoms of illness, but may transmit the virus to others through blood, semen or vaginal secretions. *AIDS (Acquired Immunodeficiency Syndrome)* is one of the late manifestations of HIV infection" [11].

HIV is not spread through causal contact. *Causal Contact* refers to contact in the workplace, school, or home. It is not intimate. More attention needs to be given to explaining what has led up to the generalization about casual contact not transmitting HIV-infection. Randall and Ashton state that

> none of the family members of the over 70,000 AIDS patients identified to date have been reported to have AIDS. Over nine different studies of family members of patients with HIV infection have failed to demonstrate HIV transmission to adults who were not sexual or needle-sharing contacts of the infected persons or older children who were not at risk from perinatal transmission [14, appendix p. 5].

MAJOR FACTORS

> Many more people (perhaps 1.5 million in the United States) are infected with HIV than have developed AIDS. In fact, many people who are infected with HIV will have no symptoms of illness for a long time-sometimes eight years or more. . . . [However,] the virus called HIV can be spread to other people [by infected persons] . . . even if they have no symptoms of illness . . . by sexual intercourse, sharing contaminated needles or from mother to infant. . . . Some people acquired HIV from infected blood transfusions before blood was screened [beginning in 1985]. . . . HIV is not spread through casual contact . . . and is not transmitted easily [10, p. 1].

Recently, HIV-infection was described as a very well-kept secret [12]. This does not occur by accident. In Minnesota, confidentiality is protected in the school by the superintendent, who keeps all information regarding an HIV/AIDS infected person in a locked file accessed only by permission of infected party and his/her parents or guardians (if the infected individual is a minor). No means which potentially could lead to breaking of confidentiality, such as duplicating or memos, should be permitted. This is essential if the school community is to be allowed access to important information. The only alternative leads to silence and ignorance. "Those who have experienced community fear and rage have stated that if they could do it all over again, they never would notify school officials about an HIV infection" [10]. It is a simple truism that the fewer people who know, the less opportunity there is for divulging information needlessly or unintentionally.

THREE OPTIONS

HIV-positive or AIDS patients have three options for dealing with public knowledge of their condition. They may:

- *Remain Totally Private*, in which case they may avoid some negative reactions, but they will also be deprived of possible positive support from the school community;
- *Decide to Share Confidential Information on a Limited Basis*, which allows support from some school staff members (whether administrators, teachers, or counselors); or
- *Choose to Make Their Condition Public*. In the last option, they, and the parents of a minor, need to give consent in writing to the school to allow the local district or school support team time to prepare for the consequences of this course of action [11].

Given the seriousness of HIV infection, there are sometimes questions about the accuracy of information.

> The Centers for Disease Control (CDC) are an important authority on HIV and AIDS. CDC epidemiologists have studied the AIDS virus since it was first reported . . . and provide a national clearinghouse for information about HIV. Most authorities consider studies and information that appear in CDC publications definitive [7, p. 33].

DEVELOPMENT OF POLICY AND AN ACTION PLAN

The HIV/AIDS policy adopted by a local school board for its district will have to accomplish many tasks. According to the Minnesota Department of Education, such a policy is expected to:

- facilitate communication among key individuals and groups around issues related to HIV infection,
- articulate the societal values of the school district and community,
- establish a plan of action in policy and procedures for dealing with a student or staff member with HIV infection and other issues which may arise,
- clearly state how federal and state laws are to be implemented in the district,
- establish a base of support to be used if questions and/or criticism arise, and
- provide a meaningful opportunity for community and school to work together to foster positive behavior which is aimed at preventing the spread of HIV [11, p. 9].

Such a district policy can be useful in other health-related areas, such as STDs other than HIV/AIDs.

Fraser includes a clear description of the *process* of policymaking. She states that the POLICYMAKING PROCESS includes ten steps:

Step 1: Gather existing information on policies, laws, and medical information. Model policies are available for examination from a variety of sources, for example, Minnesota Department of Education, *School District A.I.D.S. Policy Development: Part I: Federal and State Guidelines,* pages 11-18.

Step 2: Identify all possible sources for assistance from the local to the national level.

Step 3: Form the committee that will develop the policy including:
- a broad range of community representatives to get diverse opinions and support,
- members who are medical and legal experts
- school representatives including union and/or association representatives.

Step 4: Educate the committee and the school board about HIV infection and other pertinent issues. Elicit feelings, attitudes, and questions. It may be useful to have a presentation by an epidemiologist from state health department followed by questions and discussion.

Step 5: Identify policy issues that must be addressed. First find out which issues are already covered by federal and state laws, then develop a list of additional topics that must be addressed.

Step 6: Prepare a first draft of the policy. Have committee members share this draft with their constituencies, gather opinions, and report back to the full committee.

Step 7: Prepare the final draft of the policy.

Step 8: Present the draft to the school board. Begin the policy adoption process, which may include public hearings. Such hearings allow a broad-based opportunity for participation and can lessen possible community resistance to this policy.

Step 9: Inform the community about the policy. Hold information sessions for the media and concerned groups such as the PTA.

Step 10: Set guidelines for periodically reviewing and evaluating the policy [10, p. 28, 29].

ETR Associates' *Comprehensive Health Education Resources* of Santa Cruz, California is a clearing house for materials for HIV education [13]. *Responding With Support* includes an Individualized Health Plan for a Student with AIDS Virus Infection [14]. This also includes a chart of developmental characteristics of children and youth from ages five to nineteen on their physical, cognitive, social, self, values, and sexuality characteristics to help determine placement of curriculum concepts.

There may be some committees or teams already in place that could work on policy such as a Planning, Reporting and Evaluating Committee, Learners-At-Risk Committee, a county or community HIV Task Force, or a Community Education Advisory Committee [11]. Organizations to be represented could include the Red Cross, YMCA and YWCA because these organizations are already involved in HIV prevention.

The district policy development committee should include members from the parent organization, teachers, school nurses, student service staff, administrators from each level, student representatives from each junior and senior high school, and community members. Community representatives can be drawn from dentists, doctors, nurses, mental health professionals, clergy, law enforcement officials, public health officials, hospital administrators, wellness people from the corporate sector or community, social agencies, child protection agencies, and/or major employers of youth.

The policymaking process is an educational process which will take time, effort, flexibility, and creativity. The process may be at least as important as the policy itself. To be effective, policies need to be developed locally for this empowers people and gives them a feeling of "ownership." A multidisciplinary approach to problem solving is cited as being most productive.

There may be significant differences in the spiritual viewpoints represented in the school and community. It is vital that this planning process be conducted so that it contributes to increased understanding instead of polarization. Fraser [10] and Mann, et al. [15] specify the need to write policies in clear language so that students and community can understand. Most importantly, a policy needs to be shared effectively with the community [10, 16].

PHILOSOPHY AND POSITIVE POSSIBILITIES

One Minnesota district had a very positive response to a staff member with AIDS. The administrator interviewed felt strongly that this was due, not only to the personal qualities of the individual who was ill, but to a twenty-five-year history of openness in the district in the development of Family Life Education and other programs. Parents and students participated in these developments, and the parents retained an option of having their child excused from certain class sessions if they so chose. Currently, parents don't opt out because they've had input in course development and have a high comfort level with the course content. The school has had a peer helper group for the last five years and all segments of the school community have had considerable training about AIDS.

When the individual with AIDS chose to become public about that condition, "all there was an outpouring of love and sympathy with no negative results in the district" [16]. There was significant emotional and practical support for this person, and people remained involved up through the funeral. Concerning the presence of an HIV/AIDS person at a school, Straka continued,

> "It is not IF it's going to happen but WHEN!" . . . "A policy is only words on a sheet of paper and has no meaning without [examining] how you respond to that policy. Paramount should be the best interests of all students, parents, staff, and community".

How the policy is developed, interpreted, and taught are what really matters. This distinction is the difference between the letter of the law and the spirit of the law.

The Minnesota Department of Education "promotes strategies for positive behavior formation and behavior change which reduce risk of HIV transmission among learners . . . and contributes to a community climate which facilitates positive and diversified responses to the reality of HIV infection" [11]. Further the department advises the preparation of a school to accept a person infected with HIV so when this occurs there will be minimum disruption or interruption to education.

The thoughtful development of HIV/AIDS policies can lend objectivity to this emotionally-loaded area, defuse emotions and prevent unfortunate incidents. The policy development process may give rationale, guidance, education, support, and peace of mind. It can also prevent unfortunate incidents and eliminate the need for a public meeting to debate how a particular case will be handled.

ABSTINENCE vs "RISK REDUCTION"

> There have been difficulties in communities where people have spent undue energies debating abstinence versus risk reduction. The effect of this debate is to not spend energies on needs of students; it leaves everyone exhausted. The end goal is to protect kids and give them skills.

"The AIDS epidemic may [also] teach our society that disease prevention is more valuable than disease treatment and cure. More than 95% of health-care expenditure in the United States is for treatment rather than prevention of disease" [17].

LEGISLATION, POLICIES, GUIDELINES

Currently forty-eight states have recommendations or requirements on HIV/AIDS. Thirty states have recommendations or requirements on teaching sexual health. All states receive funding from the CDC for this area [12]. The federal laws include:

- Equal protection clause of U.S. Constitution
- Civil Rights Act of 1964
- Vocational Rehabilitation Act of 1973 : "Section 504 of the Rehabilitation Act of 1973 prohibits discrimination against individuals who have handicaps, including individuals with AIDS and/or HIV infection, as long as they are 'otherwise qualified' for their jobs" [10].
- Family Educational Rights and Privacy Act (the Buckley Amendment). This applies to government agencies and forbids anyone from revealing medical information without that person's consent. This also applies to an employee's medical information.
- Education for All Handicapped Children Act:

  > The Education for All Handicapped Children Act (Public Law 94-142) protects the right to a free and appropriate public education for students with disabilities who require special education programs. Students who are covered under this statute must both have disabilities and be in need of special education and related services. . . . Policymakers should ensure that all policies developed for students and school staff who are infected with HIV are consistent with the provisions of Section 504, P.L. 94-142 and state handicap discrimination laws and special education statutes. Otherwise, federal and state funding may be jeopardized, and the schools will be vulnerable to lawsuits [10, p. 24].

  An Individual Health Plan, an Individual Educational Plan, or an individually tailored employee plan need to be developed or changed in accordance with federal and other laws and guidelines.
- "Guidelines for Effective School Health Education to Prevent the Spread of AIDS" ((CDC) Morbidity and Mortality Weekly Report, January 29, 1988, vol. 37, S-2) incorporate principles for AIDS education that were developed by the President's Domestic Policy Council and approved by the President in 1987.

- The United States Constitution prohibits unreasonable search and seizure; the Supreme Court has ruled that taking of blood is a search. Therefore, there will be no mandatory testing for HIV virus [10, p. 18].
- The most recent "CDC Universal Precautions for Prevention of Transmission of Human Immunodeficiency Virus, Hepatitis B Virus, and Other Bloodborne Pathogens in Health-Care Settings" will be followed in cleaning up all body fluids because it is not known who is HIV infected. All staff are to be trained and demonstrate proficiency in this [10, p. 13].

In addition to federal laws and guidelines, there are state laws and guidelines relative to this area. For example, state and local laws spell out diseases to be reported, who makes the report, the content of the report, and who in the public health department receives this report. The following example of a state statute is from Minnesota.

Minnesota Statute 121.203 (Health-Related Programs)

The commissioner of education, in consultation with the commissioner of health, shall assist districts in developing and implementing a program to prevent and reduce the risk of acquired immune deficiency.

Subdivision 1: Each district shall have a program that includes at least:

(1) planning materials, guidelines and other technically accurate and updated information;
(2) a comprehensive, technically accurate and updated curriculum;
(3) cooperation and coordination among districts and Educational Cooperative Service Units;
(4) a targeting of adolescents, especially those who may be at high risk of contracting AIDS, for prevention efforts;
(5) involvement of parents and other community members;
(6) in-service training for appropriate district staff and school board members;
(7) collaboration with state agencies and organizations having an AIDS prevention or AIDS risk reduction program;
(8) collaboration with local community health services, agencies and organizations having an AIDS prevention or AIDS risk reduction program; and
(9) participation by state and local student organizations [11, p. 6].

Although state and local laws and policies will vary, these laws, policies, and guidelines dictate direction for districts and schools to follow in developing HIV/AIDS policies and addressing HIV/AIDS. The goals of Minnesota AIDS Prevention are, "The development of personal protection through active behavioral choice and caring about others through greater knowledge and understanding" [18].

ACTION PLAN TO PREVENT OR MANAGE IMMEDIATE CRISIS

1. If a staff member becomes aware of an AIDS infected student, s/he should immediately contact the building principal or superintendent. All parties should be aware of pertinent regulations concerning student privacy and documentation should be kept to document that this has been done and student rights protected.

2. A designated school official (principal, school nurse, or other appropriate staff member) should confer with a parent/guardian or, if appropriate, the student.

3. If permission is received from the parent/guardian (in writing), the designated school official should confer with the primary health care provider.

4. If no questionable behavior or medical conditions exist, appropriate district staff and/or district appointed crisis response team members should be notified. The identity of the student should be disclosed only if legally appropriate.

5. As needed (and if legally appropriate) meet with above staff members and family/student to:

   A. discuss the continuance of educational programs and the need to build a support system for the student,
   B. discuss the need for staff in-service education,
   C. discuss the need for student education,
   D. discuss the need to plan a response to possible media intrusion,
   E. to initiate a district plan for rumor control.

The superintendent needs to know if the HIV infected person has a communicable disease that can be transmitted to others (perhaps a secondary infection, such as tuberculosis) and how to plan for appropriate schooling to support person with HIV infection [10].

In addition to the steps mentioned above, the following suggestions may be pertinent:

- Act with confidence to prevent a vacuum becoming filled with destructive leadership.
- Network with other community leaders, agencies such as law enforcement, hospitals, mental health agencies, social service, crisis telephone lines.
- Make certain that confidentiality procedures are failsafe.

- "Be prepared to deliver intensive in-service and community education programs to the school/community in crisis." Take nothing for granted; use knowledgeable medical authorities, and expect to explain even "basic" information and answer questions about HIV infection and AIDS.
- "Recognize the potential minority dimensions of the issue. . . . It is important to stress that HIV is transmitted by risky behavior, not by 'risk groups.' Anyone can be infected if they engage in activities that may expose them to HIV."
- "Identify an expert in conflict resolution in case one is needed. . . . Superintendents and administrators who have already resolved AIDS-related conflicts in their communities can be particularly helpful."
- Other resources could be the state department of education, the state department of health, or a state HIV/AIDS Response Team [10, p. 31].
- It is essential that the superintendent check with the school attorney to verify that all actions are consistent with applicable laws.

Media Management

The goal here is to create a positive response and avoid sensationalism. Many people can recall unfortunate incidents glaring from the television regarding persons who are HIV infected or Persons With AIDS (PWAs). This is a "worst case scenario." The district must identify a calm, articulate spokesperson to be the sole representative of the school to the media. Administrators will have other responsibilities and will most likely not be able to take on this job with its enormous time demand. This spokesperson must be conscientiously prepared and supported thoroughly with accurate medical and legal information regarding this situation. It is the function of the media liaison to:

1. see that consistent messages are given out which will reassure the community that the situation is being handled appropriately and competently.
2. continue to build rapport with the media as well as to reinforce confidentiality and medically and legally correct information.
3. prepare press releases which state the district policies, procedures, and responses.
4. explain and reinforce the concept of casual contact and the research which supports this being no threat to the school or community.
5. indicate that *no harassment or exploitation will be tolerated.*
6. set limits concerning presence of media on school campus.

The school administration will have tasks of its own. The building principal must:

1. strive to minimize disruptions in learning.
2. prepare to facilitate support/counseling for all learners, as individuals or in small groups, who are seeking information in problem solving and decision making with regard to AIDS related issues [19].
3. provide immediate support to the HIV infected person and the family. These support measures need to incorporate the traditional counseling characteristics as well as referrals to agencies and resources associated with HIV/AIDS.
4. develop strategies to teach about how rumors are spread, their likely inaccuracies, and how to check for accurate information if that applies. This does not, however, mean to violate confidentiality or privacy. This point cannot be overlooked, it is essential that employees and students know how to handle rumors to avoid unnecessary pain for all concerned parties.

If the case of HIV/AIDS is one of public awareness, this can constitute a "teachable moment" or "teachable time" for students, staff, and community. Using a sensitive approach, without exploiting the persons involved, it could move the acknowledgement of HIV infection from cognitive awareness to affective learning of compassion, social action, and increased personal prevention and risk reduction. This requires proactive, not reactive management. The paramount goal is to minimize interruptions in learning for all students while addressing the immediate situation. "What you do now will help determine if there is a full-blown crisis or the situation is handled confidently, compassionately, and effectively" [10]. "All behavior . . . should demonstrate that AIDS poses no threat to public health by casual contact" [20]. It is wise not to assume that people understand "casual contact." There is a need to explain the concept as well as a need to explain research behind that generalization. It is crucial to demonstrate that privacy rights and strict confidentiality will be observed. The school administration must call upon the resources available such as the local response team and the state response team for assistance.

This period provides an opportunity for the entire school community to help an individual student [or staff member] reaffirm him/herself as a person. It is the response at this time that will leave a lasting impression in the minds of the HIV infected person and his/her family.

HIV EDUCATION

There is alarming evidence demonstrating the need for education in HIV prevention. For example, it is believed that over half of the adolescents are sexually active [8, 9]. Forty percent of females become pregnant before the age of twenty [17]. The STD rates indicate epidemic numbers among teens [5]. Twenty percent of people reported to have AIDS are between ages twenty and twenty-nine which suggests that many were infected while adolescents. The presence of HIV/AIDS in our population is changing as well. There are indications that infections are increasing among heterosexuals, females, and younger people [4, 9].

Erroneous beliefs are also persistent. Young people view themselves as being in monogamous relationships when, over time, they are actually practicing serial monogamy with multiple sex partners [2, 15]. Emotionally, there is the ever-present belief among teens that they will live indefinitely, coupled with the belief that they would intuitively know if something was a problem. Furthermore, there are emerging studies indicating that people do not always divulge the truth in sexual relationships [21]. Besides, "Young people often believe they are not at risk because they associate risk with belonging to a group rather than practicing certain behaviors" [15]. Research indicates that students usually know the accurate information about HIV infection and AIDS but that they do not make behavioral choices based on this information [22]. Finally, the long incubation period for HIV/AIDS is a factor in deluding people. The longer the passage of time, the less likely it is that behaviors will be associated with their consequences.

"At-risk" students are the most vulnerable to HIV infection. Research indicates that over one-third of students come from homes where there is violence, abuse, and/or alcohol/drug problems. For example, surveys show that sexual abuse occurs in grade twelve in 4 percent of the male population and 19 percent of the female population [8, 9]. These young people are the most difficult to reach by traditional education. "Many of the same adolescents are involved in antisocial behavior, alcohol and other drug use, early sexual activity, and suicide attempts. Young people at risk for any one of these are at risk for the others as well" [9]. In summary, the general adolescent population is a high risk group; however, the "at-risk" teens are significantly more vulnerable to HIV infection. Schools are required to develop programs to reach out-of-school 'at-risk' young people.

What does HIV education say to these challenges? Teens who get consistent messages from school and parents, alone or in combination, are reported less likely to be sexually active than those who do not receive such messages [9]. If teens learn to make safer choices, those behaviors could become the norm, and they may prevent the HIV epidemic from increasing. Empowerment is a core issue to facilitate persons changing from viewing themselves as powerless to being effective negotiators in relationships. *"Effective education focuses on empowerment. People never have to become infected! To empower is to protect kids and give them skills"* [12]. Classes, peer support groups, and workshops can teach negotiation skills. For example, communications with a partner could vary from superficial to thorough. Initially, teens could just reassure each other superficially that there was no cause for concern. After learning, they could discuss their concerns thoroughly and come to an agreement to practice abstinence or to make a commitment not only to monogamy but to safe sex practices. They would also become more aware that ending some relationships might be healthy.

Experiential learning will promote behavior changes. Class sessions giving the opportunity to meet HIV infected persons or AIDS patients who contracted the virus while teens could provide not just information but dialogue as well. Support groups may not only assist participants but educate them to realize that "Someone has lived this experience" [12]. Groucho Marx said he believed that life is too short to make all the mistakes yourself! Learn from someone else's mistakes because with HIV infection there may be no second chances.

HOW LONG WILL ALL THIS TAKE?

Most teachers will be quick to point out that "teaching" a class does not mean that the material has been "learned" by students. Experiencing a classroom activity does not by itself bring about a change in behavior or attitudes. "Analysis of the relationship of class hours . . . revealed that knowledge could be affected through a relatively few hours, but that significant time commitment (40 to 50 hours) is necessary to result in stable effects on attitudes and practices" [10]. Considerable student time could be spent in activities such as peer counseling, volunteering, or serving on a committee to develop programs or policies. Schools could allow students to document their hours and learning experiences and obtain school credit in social studies, health, or home economics or to fulfill the public service requirement that some states have now adopted.

Just as district policies are a form of education and most useful, educational programs need to be developed locally with peers, parents, and community participation. Schools can draw from principles for AIDS education which were developed by the President's Domestic

Policy Council and approved by the President in 1987 [10]. Guidelines are available from several resources such as GUIDELINES FOR EFFECTIVE SCHOOL HEALTH EDUCATION TO PREVENT THE SPREAD OF AIDS; MMWR Supplement, 1988, REDUCING THE RISK FOR HIV EDUCATION [7] and GENERAL PRINCIPLES FOR HIV EDUCATION [10].

The criteria for AIDS instructional materials set by the Federal Review Panel, 1989 recommends that they be technically accurate, up-to-date, gender fair, sex positive, developmentally appropriate for age, racially, ethnically, and culturally non-biased, and of sound educational methodology [23]. The guidelines for HIV/AIDS support services include experiential learning, and are sex-positive. *Sex-positive* refers to the positive perception of human sexuality which places emphasis on self-responsibility for sexual behavior. They promote the development of communication, assertiveness, and decision-making.

HIV education impacts not only students and staff but many areas in the school curriculum such as health, social studies, science, and family life education. Many of these areas may have information to contribute to HIV education. History, for example, offers insight into past epidemics and looks at the ways in which victims were treated in past health crises.

NEED FOR ASSISTANCE ON DEATH, DYING, AND GRIEF

We are reminded that as the HIV/AIDS epidemic progresses, we will all be touched by it in some way. As awareness is heightened, students and staff will need information and support in regard to such topics as denial, living preventively, terminal illness, the processes of dying, and funerals. People will need this information in order to cope with their own grief and to respond appropriately to the grief of others [2].

Grief related to HIV/AIDS can seem almost limitless. Grief will be experienced by students who have put themselves at-risk. Grief accompanies issues related to testing. And, grief follows the losses associated with the discovery that one is infected with HIV. HIV infected status will lead to grief about one's future as well as about communications with significant others. Disenfranchised grief [24]—that grief which is not publicly acknowledged or expressed—is likely to be a part of the HIV/AIDS experience and carries with it additional losses. All of this can, for some, feel like too much to bear.

As Hunter asserts, "Suicide can be triggered by a sense of loss, death, separation from friends, . . . broken relationships, loss of self-esteem or the loss of bodily integrity through illness or incapacitation and disfigurement" [25]. Since any or *all* of these may be present with HIV/AIDS, suicide prevention may need to be included as a facet of HIV/AIDS education in the schools.

Typically, sudden death necessitates a reactive school response. To plan for such a response, several questions must be answered. What policies are in place and what personnel will implement these policies? How does the cause of death effect the school response? Are there a crisis intervention team and an identified group of staff, district, and possibly community members to assist students and staff in coping? Is there follow-up with long-range planning that may be warranted? Will the media be involved concerning this death? What support will be needed from the school community by the family of the deceased?

FAMILIES IN CRISIS

Progressive illness strains the coping skills of families in which a member has AIDS. First, they must cope with the onset of disease, then preparations for death. If the PWA is a custodial parent, the issue of future custody of the children will have to be addressed. Following the death, teens and other family members need to grieve the death and to rebuild their lives. This is especially difficult for families of dying single mothers. According to recent research on healthy teens in a family where a parent has AIDS, teens often don't know the HIV status of the dying or deceased parent. Those who do know do not share that information with friends, if they do have close friends. *Over half of the families with an AIDS parent had no custody plan for the adolescent following death.* Sometimes relatives would agree to take younger children but not the adolescents [26]. With greater frequency, displaced teens are turning to schools as their last hope. The school may be the last place where a young person feels a sense of "belonging" and may asked to play a role in establishing custody, if only by the now displaced adolescent.

What will be the grief issues for the 45,600 children that are predicted to be orphaned by AIDS by 1995? [27]. These orphans, may experience overwhelming losses, and may need even more support. The children, their foster families as well as birth and adoptive families will have death-related issues that will have consequences for schools [5].

HIV and AIDS will challenge our schools to assist children, teens, and adults in death, dying and grief. The validity of courses and activities in these areas will become more apparent as the numbers of effected/infected individuals and families grows. Teacher preparation in this area will be essential. Qualities specific to death educators have been researched and are useful to consider in HIV education and support groups as well as classes on loss and death. Factors found to predict the perceived ability to help affected students include, "the ability to handle death of self, level of death anxiety, their perception of their role with students who have experienced loss, and their ability to feel comfortable in counseling grieving students" [28].

RELATIONSHIP TO CHRONIC AND LIFE-THREATENING ILLNESS

"Public concern about the HIV epidemic provides an opportunity to stress the need for districts to enact policies for handling *all* communicable diseases in the school" [10]. In districts with policies in place, this process can occur more effectively.

Schools are increasingly challenged to deal with conditions causing deaths in children and young people. The six leading causes of death for 1989 (the last year available) in ages five to fourteen are accidents, cancer, homicide and legal interventions, congenital anomalies, heart, and suicide, resulting in a total of 6,770 deaths. Among ages fifteen to twenty-four, the causes of death are accidents, homicides and legal interventions, suicide, cancer, diseases of heart, and HIV infections with a total of 31,195 [1].

Student Issues relative to life-threatening illness include:

- dealing with feelings,
- physical problems,
- confidentiality, and
- issues involving family, friends, and caregivers.

These young people will need support groups, and referrals to organizations that can assist them in coping with their diagnosis, prognosis, and specific challenges.

School Issues may include:

- confidentiality,
- privacy,
- the consequences of a specific condition for the learning process,
- prolonged absence and re-entry, and
- staff involvement and responses.

There are some similarities, as well as distinct differences, when these issues are compared with those related to HIV/AIDS. One policy will not be able to be used with all types of chronic or life-threatening illness, and a district would be wise to have at least two types of planned responses.

CONCLUSION

In the case of HIV/AIDS, a crisis plan cannot afford to be merely "reactive." There must be a proactive education-prevention dimension to any such plan. Three essential elements have been identified in effective HIV/AIDS education-prevention programs worldwide. They are:

- information and education
- health and social services
- a supportive social environment [15].

The comprehensive development of HIV policy and action plan relative to serving students and staff are mandated by federal and state laws and guidelines. They should be developed collaboratively from a positive philosophy. These policies not only involve HIV education but are related to death education and chronic and life-threatening illnesses in the schools.

The future decade requires that we continue to develop community, national, and international efforts to prevent HIV infection. The involvement of schools in the United States may ultimately span the distance between a single HIV-positive individual and efforts to turn the tide in the world-wide HIV/AIDS epidemic.

REFERENCES

1. Advance Report of Final Mortality Statistics, *Monthly Vital Statistics Report, 40*:8, Supplement 2, January 7, 1992.
2. P. H. Zalaznik, *Dimensions of Loss and Death Education (3rd Edition)*, Edu-Pac Publishing, Minneapolis, Minnesota, 1992.
3. J. Seidel, The Development of a Comprehensive Pediatric HIV Developmental Service Program, *Technical Report on Developmental Disabilities and HIV Infection, No. 7,* December 1991.
4. *Guidelines for HIV and AIDS Student Support Services,* National Coalition of Advocates for Students, Boston, Massachusetts, 1990.
5. *Caring for Children with HIV Infection, A Handbook for Foster Parents,* Minnesota Human Service Associates, St. Paul, Minnesota, 1991.
6. *Guidelines for Comprehensive Sexuality Education, K-12,* SIECUS, New York, 1991.
7. K. McCormick, *Reducing the Risk: A School Leader's Guide to AIDS Education,* National School Boards Association, Alexandria, Virginia, 1989.

8. D. W. Haffner, AIDS Education: What Can be Learned from Teenage Pregnancy Preventive Programs, *SIECUS REPORT,* August/September 1989.
9. B. Yates, *Reflections of Social Change: Minnesota Student Survey: 1989-1992,* Minnesota Department of Education, St. Paul, Minnesota, 1992.
10. K. Fraser, *Someone at School has AIDS, A Guide to Developing Policies,* National Association of School Boards of Education, Alexandria, Virginia, 1989.
11. Minnesota Department of Education, *School District A.I.D.S. Policy Development: Part I: Federal and State Guidelines,* Minnesota Department of Education, St. Paul, Minnesota, 1989.
12. R. E. Luehr, AIDS Prevention and Risk Reduction Unit of the State of Minnesota Department of Education, Interview, February 16, 1993.
13. *Comprehensive Health Education Resources 1992-1993 Catalog,* ETR Associates, Santa Cruz, California, 1993.
14. C. S. Silkworth, M. Haas, R. E. Luehr, and M. Villars, *Responding with Support: An Individualized Health Plan for a Student with AIDS/HIV,* School Nurse Organization of Minnesota and MN Department of Education, St. Paul, Minnesota, 1989.
15. J. Mann, D. J. Tarantola, and T. W. Netter (eds.) in collaboration with M. E. Cohen, Prevention, *AIDS in the World,* Harvard University Press, Cambridge, Massachusetts, pp. 325-447, 1992.
16. C. Straka, Assistant Principal of Hopkins North Junior High School, Hopkins, Minnesota, Interview, February 21, 1993.
17. B. J. Bradley, What Have School Nurses and Educators Learned from the AIDS Epidemic?, **School Nurse, 4**:1, January/February 1988.
18. Minnesota Department of Education, *AIDS/HIV Prevention in Minnesota Schools: Program Implications of the Law,* Minnesota Department of Education, St. Paul, Minnesota, 1989.
19. OSHA Regulations on Bloodborne Pathogens (29 CFR 1910 Subp. Z — Ammended), *Federal Register, 56*:235, pp. 64175-64182, December 6, 1991.
20. Northeast Metropolitan Intermediate School District 916, *The First 24 Hours: A Suggested Guide for Responding to Students Infected with the AIDS Virus,* Minnesota Curriculum Services Center, Little Canada, Minnesota, 1988.
21. G. Marks, J. L. Richardson, and N. Maldonado, Self-disclosure of HIV Infection to Sexual Partners, *American Journal of Public Health, 81*:10, pp. 1321-1322, 1991.
22. R. Fulton, *A Sociological Perspective on AIDS,* presentation at Osseo Senior High School, Osseo, Minnesota, August 28, 1991.
23. Minnesota Department of Education, *HIV/AIDS Instructional Resources for Elementary and Secondary Learners,* Minnesota Department of Education, St. Paul, Minnesota, 1992.
24. K. J. Doka, *Disenfranchised Grief: Recognizing Hidden Sorrow,* Lexington Press, Lexington, Kentucky, 1989.

25. B. E. Hunter, Adolescent Suicide: Cries for Help, *NASSP Bulletin, 72*:510, pp. 92-94, 1988.
26. B. H. Draimin, J. Hudis, and J. Segura, *The Mental Health Needs of Well Adolescents in Families With AIDS,* Planning and Community Affairs Department of the Division of AIDS Services, New York, 1992.
27. WCCO-TV, *Dimension Program on AIDS Orphans,* WCCO-TV: Minneapolis, Minnesota, February 21, 1993.
28. A. L. Cullinan, Teachers' Death Anxiety, Ability to Cope with Death, and Perceived Ability to Aid Bereaved Students, *Death Studies, 14*:2, pp. 147-160, 1990.

BIBLIOGRAPHY

Clearinghouse for Materials, Videos, Network Publications/ETR Associates, Santa Cruz, California, 1993.

HIV Infection and AIDS, The American National Red Cross, May 1989.

HIV Infection and Developmental Disabilities, Brookes Publishing Company, Baltimore, Maryland, 1991.

Minnesota Department of Education, *School District A.I.D.S. Policy Development: Part II: Resources,* Minnesota Department of Education, St. Paul, Minnesota, 1989.

Moffatt, B. C., *When Someone You Love has AIDS: A Book of Hope for Family and Friends,* IBS Press, Santa Monica, California, 1986.

Rogers, M., et al., Lack of Transmission of Human Immuno-deficiency Virus from Infected Children to their Household Contacts, *Pediatrics, 85*:2, pp. 210-214, February 1990.

Schools Systems and AIDS: Information for Teachers and School Officials, The American Red Cross, November 1988.

U.S. Office for Substance Abuse Prevention, *How Getting High Can Get You AIDS (PHD573),* U.S. Office for Substance Abuse Prevention, Washington, D.C., 1991.

U.S. Office for Substance Abuse Prevention, *Preventing HIV Infection among Youth (BK193),* U.S. Office for Substance Abuse Prevention, Washington, D.C., 1991.

CHAPTER 8

Preparing the School Community to Cope with Violence

William Lee, Jr.

Preparing the school community to cope with crises is an important topic and worthwhile focus for a helping book. One crisis which is increasingly appearing in schools is that of violence.

THE CONTEXT OF VIOLENCE

Unfortunately, violence as an issue, occupies many hours of my thoughts on an almost daily basis. The more I think about it, the more complicated and multidimensional the problem becomes. Many written approaches suggest methods of responding or reacting to violence without addressing or reviewing the context in which it occurs. The context of violence is important for it provides us with a perspective. It also highlights the complexities and contradictions inherent in understanding violence, both of which are central to coping with the phenomenon. Additionally, the contradictions and complexities of violence require "mega-sorting," enmeshing oneself in, proceeding through and then emerging from this mental quagmire with a glimmer of understanding. That one iota of insight can lead us to a broad understanding of the phenomena of violence.

Several questions present a starting point for our inquiry;

1. what is the nature and what are the parameters of violence?
2. what is my/our/your philosophical perspective about humankind and violence?
3. what approaches are best to simplify such a fluid topic with its multiple pathways?

4. what are the immediate concerns relative to any discussion on violence? and
5. what is violence and what is it not?

Let us now consider these questions.

WHAT IS VIOLENCE?

Violence is complex. As an expression of our national character it tops every problem list of our cities and towns. Violence is like a virus eating at the very fabric of our society. As a nation, we have failed to recognize the nature and negative impact that violence has upon our society. It is attacking our national well being to such an extent that it has been declared a public health epidemic by the National Center for Disease Control.

PATHS OF UNDERSTANDING

There are three pathways which we must travel to understand the problem of violence.

PATH ONE is to demystify violence, whose appearance is sometimes elusive and abstract. It is as if we were tracking footprints in desert sands, only to have the footprints appear and then disappear. The context I establish seeks not to condemn, condone, apologize, nor protest but to provide a way to understand and to view human behavior. Human behavior is best understood in its socio-environmental context.

To suggest ways to prepare the school community to cope with violence we must first explore the underlying causes of violence. An immediate signpost directs us to explore what exactly violence is and what are its underlying causes.

Violence is not necessarily understood by studying only its end result. Violence is about power and control; trying to get or maintain it, the lack of it, and/or the loss of it. Violence does not occur in a vacuum. To understand its causes, we must first examine the components of violence and the resulting carnage. What we see is a picture of abandonment, violation, deprivation, helplessness and loss. We must be conscious of the forces which contribute to a human being's willingness to do violence—physical and psychological harm—to another. Proactively, our first hurdle is to avoid becoming part of the problem.

VIOLENCE: A PERSPECTIVE

A central theme to understanding and reducing violence is that violent behavior is firmly established within the human repertoire. It emerged as a by-product of our ancestors' struggles to imprint species dominance on this planet. Using violence has become an established human response to perceived challenges and threats to survival. The record of human behavior suggests that, from deep within our brain, conflict resolution elicits violence as an instinctive method of response. Conflict resolution without violence requires re-learning. It will be necessary to teach humankind new methods of communicating about and/or coping with problems. This perspective is evolutionary, a view that humankind is always "becoming." We are continually growing and not necessarily chained to a history of violence. We are capable of growth beyond our present condition. We have the spirit and will necessary to accomplish this human transformation. However, this transformation will require new approaches to handling human conflict and problem solving. Society's increased awareness and reaction to violence and our desire to find alternatives provide humankind with a window of opportunity. It provides an opportunity to directly influence the ways we resolve conflict. This approach moves humans from basic survival tactics (the fight or flight response) and prepares us for our journey along humankind's evolutionary path toward "becoming." This is a process similar to the metamorphosis of the caterpillar-to-butterfly which will not only bring about a cessation of violence but will bring with it a positive and permanent change. This change can produce a type of human behavior that leads to team and group cooperation, a type of thinking needed to energize society into the 21st century.

What are the parameters of violence? What is the extent of its influence on other events? We are concerned with understanding the range of influence, the depth of reactions and the vibrations or ripple effects of violence. These are some of the questions we must consider as we move along the pathways leading to an understanding of violence.

PATH TWO is a review of some seldom considered influences to physical displays of violence. It is difficult to present or comment on violence without a review of the many factors in our society that influence a violent outcome. However, what are most often overlooked are the major factors leading to the physical manifestation of violence. I recently saw on the front page of a major Boston newspaper a picture of an American F-14 Fighter pilot. The headline said "Saddam Gets a Spanking." The caption beneath the picture referred to a mission to bomb Iraqi targets. However, the picture showed the pilot's right hand raised, bent at the elbow, with a gun in his hand. I wondered if the pilot was also going to shoot at Iraqi targets from miles away in the sky? I thought about the display of this gun in the hands of a "hero," about Boston's cities and towns inundated with guns and about the violent behavior associated with guns. Without conscious intent, it was as though the picture reinforced the handgun as a type of "conflict resolution," this time on an international scale. This example reflects only a small part of the typical climate in which we attempt to understand the reasoning behind the increase in violent behavior and guns to solve disputes in our society.

PATH THREE asks what is violence? Our society is a living, growing entity influenced by the behavior of others and the acceptance of that behavior by those in power. It was mentioned earlier that violence is a product of power and control relationships. By the time we see the physical manifestation of violence there has been invisible structural and psychological violence done to those whom we now see as perpetrators. To understand violent behavior we must walk same pathways as those who use violence to communicate. Why is violence their way to resolve conflict?

Our national leaders are in a position to provide guidance, mold the national psyche and define moral codes. How do we, on the national level, ultimately resolve conflict? Are we willing to use force and violence to get what we want? Do we truly believe that "the end justifies the means?" Is there any substance to the charge that we are "global bullies"? What are the influences and messages sent by our leadership about the national resolve in conflict relationships? What are the implied messages about violence?

What types of messages are produced when TV, other media, and computer games' central themes are "seek out and destroy," "kill or be killed?" American television provides more references to violence than other forms of media and transmits violent programming around the world. The main objective is to destroy the villain and the more violent the methods employed, the more popular the show. Violent behavior is rewarded and the perpetrator of the most successful violent action is the "winner." This person then becomes someone who is worshipped and admired as a hero. Are there any messages about acceptable behaviors?

Is it violence when corporate mergers and bank manipulations plunder and raid the public's monetary trust causing victims to cash in social and entitlement programs to pay the tab? What messages are sent when law enforcement personnel, sworn to uphold the law violate it by brutalizing citizens solely on the basis of skin color or different cultural backgrounds? How do our senior citizens describe behaviors associated with pension, life, and retirement savings that are stolen through bank fraud or the savings and loan fiasco? When a mother is made to choose between fuel or food for her children, is that an act of violence? Children raising children, abandoned and throw-away children, children selling sexual favors to survive, dead-beat dads, urban blight, chronic unemployment, drug abuse, sexual and physical assault, racism and classism. What are these? Are these acts of violence?

Violence is a learned response to a perception or feeling that your safety or your life is threatened. This creates a way of acting which has limited options. Given the above transgressions, the individual experiences the world with a view that it is a hostile, aggressive, unsafe place which is continually violent toward him/her. "I only carry this gun to feel safe and protect myself. I am not the violent one."

To deny equal access by not providing, or purposely with-holding, resources needed by an individual erodes competence, lowers self-esteem and arrests development of basic social skills. It is often easier to use violence than to cope with the stress of seeking alternatives to resolve interpersonal conflicts. Is it violence, when education, housing, resources, political and social clout and geographic location are used against a group of people solely on the basis of color, class, cultural and/or socio-economic difference? If gender and sexual preference issues are used to determine an individual's monetary, social and/or human worth, is that violence?

Historically, by the time law enforcement, social service agencies and the general public focus on a problem of violence, the perpetrator has been conditioned by repeated acts of violence upon them. For many young people, our schools and the people in them are seen as just another group that seeks to make them "victims."

We have a society where we face daily disillusionment because many everyday role models are unavailable or destroyed. The peer group with its gang mentality has become the crisis response team for our youth. Physical violence for turf control and conflict resolution takes place daily. We are in a place where young people's concerns are only about today. They live for the moment. There are no dreams or hopes about the future, for them that future has already vanished.

As we moved along our three paths, we could see some of the complexity of violence. Violence does not always show itself physically nor does it occur in a vacuum. Before physical violence occurs there are precipitating issues and there are many contradictions inherent in the basic perspective of what is or is not violence.

WHO ARE THESE CHILDREN?

Who are these children in our classrooms? They are children who have observed violent, physical assault and who have suffered other violent losses. Upon first glance we might expect to see a saddened, depressed, and perhaps a tearful expression. On the contrary, what is observed are the masks covering the hurt, confusion, self-fragmentation, structural disorganization, and pain. These masks are deeply fortified against external penetration and exposure yet internally they are thin protective veils and offer the major keys to the individual's behavior and control mechanisms. Once the masks are lifted or removed, the rage underneath is so disorganized and uncontrollable that its energy and power can appear to be beyond human cognitive restraints. It is within this context that I present the Imploded Child.

Imploded children are those who have been victimized, who have experienced violent losses and who possess hidden rage and explosive anger. In a classroom, these children present a facade that is uncaring, cold and distanced when met with a discussion or situation of loss. They smile and laugh when talking about violence and violent death of friends. Unfortunately, because of this misunderstanding, these children may experience the withdrawal of empathy and compassion by teachers. Empathy and compassion are what these children need most. The consequences of this misunderstanding by those who interact and work with these children are long-term and severe. These are the children who are having children. It is these "throw-aways" and abandoned children who are creating without intervention another generation of the same.

The way these children handle major loss is a method that helps them stay in control. These children and teens often state that to acknowledge the loss would bring them in touch with that part of the self behind the vail: the enraged and confused self. The peer culture in the inner-city classroom does not respect outward displays of empathy and compassion. This is not permitted because it connects others with feelings they too cannot control. Peers are fearful of exposing themselves and their feelings and seek to create an environment where there is no risk of this happening.

Teachers also fear dealing with anger because it may unlock and release their own unresolved rage. Control is an American obsession and the thought of losing control is met with immediate distancing and denial. In the classroom, any student who signals or hints at the expression of anger is met with the message that it is inappropriate to express anger. If a student is not capable of suppressing this emotion, he/she may be identified as a "problem."

Usually children who have been physically or sexually assaulted and also those who have experienced loss from a violent death may have had little or no opportunity to safely express or externalize feelings of anger, violation and/or abandonment. Over a period of time they become victims of the fear of internal upheaval. There is anxiety associated with their ability to keep a lid on this powerful emotion.

These children need opportunities to communicate with others who have had similar experiences. When that occurs they can observe within others a part of themselves. They can then understand what is a "normal" reaction to an "abnormal" situation. Healing can begin with the sharing of experiences, speaking about the unspeakable, empowering the self to name those events, making meaning of the meaningless. There is a chance to learn from each other to cope with their feelings, and for schools and teachers provide a safe place with clear boundaries.

Once anger is properly elicited teachers can coach children, through role play situations, in the practice of verbal or artistic expression of feelings of loss. This offers an alternative to physical expression, often through violence, of the feelings connected to those losses.

A review of the questions and pathways set forth above provides a framework for understanding the type of environment within which we exist. This understanding provides us with some perspective on the conditions we face as we attempt to prepare school community to cope with violence.

WHAT SHALL WE DO?

What shall we do to cope with the increase in violence? It is my belief that we need to inform, support and prepare the school community to cope with this crisis.

It is good to have a healthy respect for scholarly rigor and methodologically sound approaches. However, helping schools prepare and implement crisis protocols requires more than intellectual approaches laden with technical jargon. In a practical and empathic spirit, without rejecting research oriented works, we must work within a socio-environmental context to view human behavior associated with violence. Note that this approach purposely avoids presenting a step-by-step approach for implementing and promoting violence prevention and non-violent resolution of conflict within schools. I do not believe that human behaviors and issues are best understood in some kind of linear, step by step progression of what constitutes an appropriate method for communicating information to all students. Underneath it all is a firm belief that understanding the experience and effects of violence upon persons, especially children who become adults, requires some empathy and compassion for their situations and a willingness to validate their experiences. Second, my approach is task based—operating and guided primarily by the question "what are the tasks associated with preparing school communities to cope with conveying information to this particular type of student?"

There are several tasks associated with the above:

1. understanding the effects, developmentally and emotionally, of violence on children;
2. understanding the nature and effects of the circle of violence, particularly upon those associated with and working with victims on a daily basis;
3. understanding and recognizing secondary victimization (vicarious traumatization), and
4. understanding communities, especially knowing that communities are living, dynamic, biological environments which cultivate certain qualities in their members.

This chapter does not attempt to provide definitive statements on violence and crisis intervention in schools because of the uniqueness of each community. This chapter shall present ideas, feelings and concerns predicated upon my work and experiences in urban schools, in actual violence prevention and recovery programs, community crisis intervention and crisis response teams, conducting counseling and training workshops, international and national presentations on violence and loss and from discussions with others like ourselves who are concerned about the proliferation of violence in our homes, communities and schools. I wish to engage the reader, hopefully, in ongoing thought and dialogue about issues of prevention, intervention and postvention methods of dealing with violence.

THE COMMITMENT TO HELP

A central plea resonates throughout this chapter. It is one which encourages teachers and school personnel to have the commitment and the will to help our young people, especially children from traumatized inner-city communities, think and use methods other than violence in conflict resolution. This acknowledges the fact that in high crime/high profile urban communities, the last thing one wants is to be is different. Non-violent viewpoints are not inner-city community norms. Non-violent viewpoints and actions are certain to identify those who display this behavior as different. This will make the task a difficult one, however, our commitment and resolve to help young people must remain unchanged.

Preparing school communities to cope with violence requires an extensive administrative commitment which recognizes the effect that violence has upon children's educational readiness, classrooms and learning environments and the society at large. What is required is an administration which demonstrates support for school wide initiative and resolve. This administration must make a commitment to help its students understand and internalize pathways toward non-violent resolution of conflict by presenting strategies of coping for those individuals who are witnessing and living with daily violence. School administrators must encourage collaboration with, and assign priority to, the efforts of *all* school personnel; the superintendent, principal, counselors and teachers. Superintendents must demonstrate this priority through their daily behavior. Their action and communication must always support efforts to integrate concepts and ideas about coping with violence and violence prevention into the school curriculum. Leadership must come from principals who vigorously promote these approaches within their schools. Enthusiasm shown by a superintendent for a pedagogical concept usually signals an emphasis within the individual schools. School-based leadership through the principal will motivate teachers to introduce the concepts within their classroom curriculum. Teachers who acquaint themselves with the everyday violence that their students are exposed to should be able to look to their administrators and find encouragement for taking action. Through classroom involvement teachers can come to appreciate the pain, frustration, and victimization that young people, especially those of the inner-city, experience daily. Also, teachers might begin to understand that many minority, inner-city students come to school afflicted by the fears, uncertainties and traumas that plague their parents. These students are already exhibiting the behaviors and appearance of persons with a history of violence perpetrated against them. They display coping behaviors designed to protect themselves against further actual and/or perceived victimization. Teachers and school personnel must be alert to the reality of the student's situation without stripping that student of all survival skills that are utilized within that environment. Before observing and labeling the child as violent, it is necessary to understand that the community may be violent. Therefore, we must help the student to understand first, that they are being victimized and second, the psychological implications of that victimization.

Teachers must be constantly aware of their interactions within the school environment, because children constantly observe and evaluate them. For example, if teachers walk by students daily and do not speak and have no concern for the environment being created by their actions, it may be perceived by students as the perpetuation of a hoax. "Teachers are only here for a paycheck, they don't care about me/us." This is yet another act of violence.

A BASIC UNDERSTANDING

Schools are communities within communities. Preparing a school community to cope with violence requires knowledge of the community makeup and the circles of influence incorporated in it. We must consider the context and culture of the communities who send us their children. Children are in and of that community and the meaning making systems employed by them are reflections of those of the greater community as a whole. How do they understand? How do they learn? What are their experiences? These are the questions which must be considered and the attempted answers are the foundation upon which education is established.

For example, during play, children will act out the qualities and most "admired" characteristics of their environment. It is these "sanctioned" qualities which the children bring to bear in their school environment. Displays of these behaviors are not necessarily bad if we use them as "teachable moments."

These are children from traumatized communities where adults and role models are fragmented, psychologically not available, angry, or desensitized to violence themselves. This results in disorganized, emotionally confused and non-unified structures.

An understanding of these issues is required for educating and determining the learning readiness and the availability of a unified and complete child to receive instruction.

Educational interventions into these young people's lives must demonstrate an understanding and willingness to go beyond transmission of information and knowledge. These children must be engaged at non-verbal, core levels. They must be allowed and encouraged to reconnect with humanity through teachers who validate and empower these children and re-work their fragile and fractured emotional structures. Therefore it is essential that educators understand and demonstrate compassion and empathy towards these children. In doing so, educators will create a learning environment which addresses most of these children's first concern: it is not what the teacher knows, it is whether the teacher cares. This understanding is fundamental in order to engage any child.

RESPONSIBILITY TO THE FUTURE

Institutions that train educators and the educators themselves must have a dialogue and together define the mission of teaching. We can no longer, if we want to be relevant to today's children, define school and teaching by the roles, functions and standards of the 1950s. The world has changed. Teaching and the teacher must broaden the roles and goals to acknowledge issues with which today's society grapples. The institutions established for providing guidance to our youth must help address the critical issues confronting them and coping with violence is a major one. The teaching profession cannot remain the same. Teachers can no longer avoid these issues with comments such as "I am only here to teach English", "I was not trained as a social worker" or "That's student support/guidance department's problem, I am hired to teach reading." We must collaborate, become part of the team, an active member of the group. Our functions increasingly overlap in every area of a child's life. Today there are no rigid boundaries. Teaching children effectively requires a view of the whole child and if a part of the child is dysfunctional it is going to affect those areas which are the educator's primary areas of influence and/or instruction. We must show a genuine interest in developing and caring about our children and not only dealing with the items in our job descriptions or those for which we receive a paycheck. Our children are responding to our behaviors not to our words. They are doing as we do, not as we say. At the bottom line, our lip service to caring about them is the major reason we are losing them. They do not want to be a part of the hypocrisy endemic within their parent's generation. Schools must redefine their mission to include sharing in the development of humans who function as team members. Schools must promote non-violent behavior as an acceptable mode for resolving human conflicts. Schools must help shape and prepare minds to compete and drive the world of the next century. The roles and the way we relate to each other is of the utmost importance as we embark upon space exploration and other challenges of the future. Our responsibility in raising our children requires an acceptance on our own part of non-violent resolution of crises.

As machines take over and other human functions are limited in the workplace, the world's continual safety may hinge on cooperative performance and non-violent resolution of disagreement. Schools involved in preparing young minds for the future can assist in helping implement a non-violent approach as these young people come of age.

PREPARING SCHOOLS

No single chapter can attempt to resolve all the issues highlighted as factors associated with violence. However, we can explore one issue in depth: the school environment itself.

Any violence prevention/intervention program suggested for schools must consider the climate in which these programs are implemented. The reader is reminded to always reflect upon the established phenomena of violence.

I will use the urban inner-city school community as the focal point of preparing a school community to cope with violence: an educational and curriculum based approach. When inner-city communities are used as examples, other types of communities (suburban, rural) often try to deny or minimize the extent and reach of violence. There is a false sense of security exhibited by comments such as "that only happens in the ghetto," "we don't have things that bad" or "those elements don't live here." We cannot continue to minimize the societal impact of violence as it increases and escalates by using coping statements such as it was an "isolated situation." We must accept that violence is right next door and may well appear in our own homes. Domestic violence, violent rape, suicide, child molestation and job related murder has become as much a part of rural, small town America as it has in the urban, metropolitan city. I am not prepared to differentiate (and I would not attempt to try) among types of violence. There are no "better" or "worse" acts when violence involves human suffering, just ask the victim on the receiving end of any sort of violence.

WHAT IS NECESSARY

Preparing school communities to cope with and address the needs of students who are victims of or observers of violence requires implementation of some type of violence prevention/intervention program within the school community.

There are many issues that must be addressed in order to implement an effective program. Training and treatment must be comprehensive. All components of the school community: classroom atmosphere, educational processes, curriculum content, ancillary service providers, school personnel, parents and students must be integrated into such a program.

THE TOOLS WE HAVE

How do we teach our children, what types of experiences do we provide for them? How do we teach them to resolve conflict through non-violent resolution? How much of the school curriculum deals directly with the phenomenon of violence? These factors shall directly affect the content and teaching of violence prevention in the school community. The classroom is the major learning environment within the school. We must begin any prevention attempt by focusing in on the classroom.

THE SCHOOL ENVIRONMENT– ITS POTENTIAL

Children utilize play as the key expression of their ideas and concerns. They become competent by practicing what we call "child's play" until a situation is mastered. The classroom is a microcosm of the community. The interaction, views, behaviors and actions reflect the values and beliefs of the community outside its walls. A classroom where the teacher values the uniqueness in each child is a model which children can use toward each other in their daily interactions. The classroom's operation provides human interaction which may not be demonstrated at home or in the neighborhood. Early positive interpersonal relations are beginning steps toward counteracting violence. These early experiences can become tools in conflict resolution. The classroom experience may be the only opportunity that children have to test different methods of resolving conflicts. A positive classroom experience may provide necessary hope.

Paraphrasing an old Chinese proverb, a child, like a piece of paper, is subject to and becomes the product of those marks placed upon him/her. If we do not want children to become violent, hostile, oppressive, and/or aggressive in solving disagreements we must teach them consideration and respect for themselves and for others. For example, children with a high level of self-esteem seldom display violence in resolving disputes. I often hear neighborhood teens greeting each other with the phrase, "Increase the peace." This suggests more than a passive approach to the problem of violence. It suggests taking action. The pathways to cooperation may begin with adults who treat children with respect and consideration in everyday situations. However, children must be taught to take responsibility for their actions, to be self-motivated and to treat peers fairly and non-violently.

We must, as much as humanly possible, provide school environments beginning with classrooms free of humiliation, intimidation and fear. Schools, and in particular individual classrooms, are some of the few places that can provide emotionally safe places for children. With some guidance and limit setting, there are opportunities to make conscious and controllable those hidden, intense and highly charged emotions that fuel an emotional nature. An environment that demonstrates fairness and justice and where discipline fosters growth and cooperation does not use controlling devices against children and adults. This is a classroom where children are willing to explore and to review critically their reality while considering other possibilities. It is important that we use the children's (and our own) energy to create these opportunities and to come up with other ways to use the classroom beneficially. Just the fact that opinions are allowed, openness encouraged and talking about a problem is okay provide much needed relief for children in the class.

Young children absorb information from their surroundings rather unconsciously. Internally the school classroom can contribute to violence prevention by passively constructing messages which teach non-violence. Pictures, books, videos, and situations which depict non-violence and cooperation convey a message. Storytelling, art and role playing situations, where the hero solves problems using non-violent methods, can also be used. A child's lifestyle as well as exposure to television may contradict the classroom message and approach. The media often demonstrate that violence is the operating norm in conflict resolution. Our classroom approaches should present another point of view, one which demonstrates non-violence and cooperation as acceptable options to human conflict. Additionally, for upper grades, we can incorporate homework assignments, research papers, discussion groups and class presentations focusing on the *power* of non-violence as shown by the lives of Gandhi and Martin Luther King. Another valuable activity which connects home and school is a take-home assignment which encourages discussion about violence and non-violence. At the very least we can provide the child with an opportunity to open discussion at home of the topic of violence. The school may use awards to recognize those students who resolve, or help others in the school community to resolve, conflicts non-violently. The class can create an award which identifies a community organization or individual who has contributed to a decrease in conflict, crime, or violence in the neighborhood. This helps convey positive attitudes about the community. This can offer hope by informing everyone of *positive* actions. It offers support by showing that there are others working to solve the problems of violence. If all elements of the school community cooperate, "increasing the peace" *can* become an accepted norm.

CREATING A "SAFE" PLACE WITHIN THE SCHOOL

An immediate, specific step for every school would be the creation of a "safe" place that allows a space for student "reflection." Ideally, this would be a private, permanent area decorated and used by all individuals in the school community. It can offer a safe haven for the sharing of concerns, problems, and ordeals. It can be staffed by community volunteers, teachers, peer support, guidance counselors, and student support team members. This space should be open before classes begin, throughout the day, and for some time after classes end, as long as there are stusdents in the building. If possible, there should also be a phone number posted for students to call during emergencies at night or on weekends. This should be a space available to all children/students where they can share personal issues which are confronting them. These issues may be creating anxiety, poor attendance or poor overall school performance. This place and these people may be able to provide a moment in the day that will help a student to pull it together or hold it together emotionally. It should not necessarily replace, or try to be, a counseling or therapy center. It should follow a crisis debriefing model where the individual can focus on the meaning of an event for them, acknowledge the event and sort it out or get in touch with feelings associated with the event. It is hoped that once a situation is acknowledged and feelings are identified the individual may become less confused, more able to tolerate any remaining confusion. He/she may be able to maintain a greater feeling of personal control and then prepare in a calm manner to take action. This can decrease the likelihood of acting prematurely and can encourage alternatives to violence by allowing students to get in touch with their emotions.

THE ROLE OF THE TEACHER

Perhaps the most important and potentially powerful role model for violence prevention is the classroom teacher. Since violence is a learned behavior, teachers can help prevent violence through their daily interaction with children. Teachers have an opportunity to teach children how to deal with anger and to help children find ways to vent their angry feelings. There must be initial staff training and continuous in-service follow-up showing a variety of methods for teaching non-violent conflict resolution. It must be remembered that, when dealing with emotionally intrusive subjects like violence, teachers are exposed to a secondary circle of victimization. Therefore, special requirements are necessary for programs that prepare direct-contact educators for any such program.

Teachers, like their students, are whole beings with personal as well as professional needs. These personal needs are equally valid and must be considered when asking teachers to adjust and incorporate new materials into their repertoire. We must allow teachers to explore those needs and provide time for such efforts. These discussions should ask: what type of information is needed; what administrative support will be required; and what type of peer support can be expected on a group or individual level? We cannot expect teachers to be available as whole complete human beings unless we provide materials and training to meet their identified needs and continue to support their continued growth and development as they undertake this approach.

In a violence prevention program, teachers need a knowledge of developmental issues, of the effects of trauma on children and a knowledge of methods that are helpful in helping these children to heal. We must move beyond acquisition of subject-centered knowledge and proficiencies. We need teachers with a working knowledge of what is developmentally appropriate, given these conditions and these children. Teachers need to know what risk factors are present in specific groups of children. Teachers must master techniques which will help them to impart coping and non-violent resolution skills to children who are facing an almost daily barrage of violence. Because of the importance of this work, training in violence prevention techniques must become incorporated into the training of all personnel serving in our schools.

It is important in teacher preparation to allow educators an opportunity to explore and express their own issues and experiences with violence. This increases the possibility that an individual can become aware of and deal with personal issues in a conscious way before unconsciously allowing them to have an impact on their young charges. Past relationships which may include victimization, or observation of violence, should be identified and worked out by the educator. With awareness of personal issues, educators are then free to help others without personal issues intruding. This approach can increase teacher comfort and competence levels when working toward violence prevention.

IMPLEMENTING A VIOLENCE-PREVENTION PROGRAM

Any effective intervention strategy must allow for teacher flexibility in developing a "comfortable" approach to the topic. Efforts at implementation should include schools, businesses, city officials, community leaders, parents, and students. Representation of these groups in intervention programs would positively reinforce a spirit of cooperative effort. If we look back at the issues raised at the start of this chapter, we can see that any effort to address the issue of violence requires a broad-based community involvement. Increased funding will, most likely, not be available so these programs will need to use creative approaches to reach their goal.

The following illustrate the level and type of involvement necessary from each group.

School Involvement

- should establish and coordinate in-service training for teachers and administrators,
- utilize training programs that focus on classroom activities which are developmentally appropriate and psychologically and educationally sound for teaching violence prevention.

Business Involvement

- should develop partnerships with the schools,
- allow employees who volunteer, including those who are related to students, to act as a school-business liaison.

City/Community Involvement

- should include social service agencies, youth and street workers, recovery program members, college students and senior citizens to form pools of volunteers which can help with supervision at school sites.

Parent Involvement

- should use available parents as a labor pool to assist their children,
- draw on individuals who must work in order to be eligible for welfare benefits, but have been unable to find employment in the private sector.

Student Involvement

- should train a cadre of young people to assist with peer counseling and mediation, support services, and situational violence prevention seminars.
- be used to staff the "safe" room in each school.

Creating partnerships among these different groups brings a variety of perspectives and possible solutions to the problem of violence and to each specific crisis which might arise.

CRISIS INTERVENTION

Violence effects every sector within our society. (Editor's note: As this chapter was being finished an explosion ripped through New York's World Trade Center. Several people died and over a thousand were injured. Whatever the cause of the blast, there are literally tens of thousands of young people throughout the New York metropolitan area and across the country whose lives will now be different due to a very personal fear that violence can "explode" upon their lives or those of their loved ones at any unguarded moment. The terrorism that has effected so many children around the world has now seemingly reached our shores.) At some time or other all schools will have to deal with incidents of violence in or around their sites. No school is insulated and administrators who think otherwise are creating an atmosphere ripe for disaster. It is recommended that schools do *not* wait for violence to occur before creating a response plan.

A RESPONSE PLAN FOR SCHOOLS

Level I

The first steps in creating such a plan are:

1. to develop an understanding of the nature of violence and the complexity of the issues involved.
2. to recognize that both the perpetrator and victim of violence are similar since the violence visited upon the victim is often a continuation of prior violence in the life of the perpetrator.
3. to understand that violence creates many victims and that those who appear to be "bystanders" can be important factors in the escalation or deescalation of violence.

Level II

The next phase of preparation involves recognizing that violence can occur at any time. In order to plan for the day it does, schools should:

1. conduct a *Violence Information Meeting* of all school personnel and community groups where:
   - volunteers will be recruited to form crisis response teams, including educators, community members, media representatives, police, medical personel, and parents.
   - hypothetical situations can be addressed, guidelines formed and possible responses planned.
2. form a *Crisis Response Team* which will:
   - categorize issues and set priorities for actions to be taken in response to crisis,
   - develop a communication system to inform teachers and key community personnel and control rumors while avoiding alarming students unnecessarily.
   - establish the leaders and assign roles to each team member,
   - create *general* guidelines and strategies for crisis response based on particular school and community needs.
   - conduct practice sessions during which the steps of crisis response are acted out (in much the same way that schools conduct regular fire drills),
   - continue training sessions for educators and community members.

The crisis intervention model developed in the mental health disciplines has been found to be most helpful in thinking through crisis intervention in schools. This model views intervention efforts as primary, secondary and tertiary. In adapting it to a violence prevention program the following guidelines may be used:

Primary Intervention provides activities which can help prevent a crisis from happening, including:
- storytelling, art role play (with non-violent themes),
- discussion of feelings, especially anger,
- activities highlighting contributions of diverse ethnic and cultural groups,
- collaboration with groups from the outside community.

Secondary Intervention includes actions which react quickly to a crisis to stop its escalation and prevent it from spreading to bystanders, including:
- school-wide practice in crisis response,
- formation of a Crisis Response Team,
- establishing a crisis/rumor phone line with direct access to an administrator or designated response team leader,
- utilize crisis response team members outside of the school to meet with young people on the streets.

Tertiary Intervention includes activities which provide assistance to persons who have experienced a crisis to help control and limit possible negative long-term consequences, including:

- establish and maintain a school-based reflective ("safe") space,
- offer individual, on-site counseling and group counseling,
- use a critical incident stress debriefing model to offer regular debriefing sessions for students and for staff members.

It is important to remember that this plan can be used with or extend what has already been established or is currently in operation in a school. You do not need to start from scratch. Incorporate information which is helpful and discard that which does not "fit."

CONCULSION

We have followed our path to its end. We began by looking at the context of violence. We moved on to attempt to clarify what we mean by violence. We attempted to demystify violence and to look beyond its physical manifestation to reframe it in terms of power and control. We identified links between perpetrators and victims of violence and saw that each has suffered in an ongoing pattern of violence.

Moving on to the school setting, we saw that it may well be necessary to reshape our schools traditional patterns of response and to help teachers and community members to prepare to take on new responsibilities if violence prevention is to be successful in the schools. Finally, some possible responses for schools are offered in the form of suggested guidelines.

Violence is an epidemic infecting our society. The cure to an illness can frequently be found by examining its obverse. Solutions which draw on collaboration and cooperation are the obverse of violent response. We sometimes pay less attention to the obvious and mundane examples of that type of collaboration and cooperation—in a family, among siblings, in churches, clubs, rap or rock groups, in sports teams, gangs or other societal groups. We need to find them where they are and to build on the successes they may have already claimed. Any play must draw on the ability of all of its actors if it is to succeed.

Violence in our society is not new. Nothing new is required to face it, other than our acknowledgement of responsibility for ourselves as adults and for our children.

BIBLIOGRAPHY

Ammerman, R. T. and M. Herson, eds., *Treatment of Family Violence: A Sourcebook,* Wiley, New York, 1990.

Achenbach, T., *Developmental Psychopathology,* Wiley, New York, 1982.

Bowlby, J., *Attachment and Loss: Attachment (Vol. I),* Basic Books, New York, 1969.

Bowlby, J., *Attachment and Loss: Separation (Vol. II),* Hogarth Publishers, London, England, 1973.

Erikson, E., *Childhood and Society,* Norton, New York, 1950.

Garbarino, J., et al. *Children in Danger: Coping With the Consequences of Community Violence,* Jossey-Bass, San Francisco, California, 1992.

Hankins, G., *Prescription for Anger: Coping With Angry Feelings and Angry People,* Princess, Beaverton, Oregon, 1988.

Morgan, J. D., *Helping Those At Risk,* King's College, London, Ontario, 1987.

Lee, W., *Without Empathy and Compassion: At Risk and Protective Factors of Violence Among Black and Latino Adolescents,* unpublished paper presented at the 2nd International Conference on Children and Death at the University of Edinburgh, Scotland, 1992.

Leenaars, A. A., *Life Span Perspectives of Suicide,* Plenum Press, New York, 1991.

Kegan, R., *The Evolving Self,* Harvard University, Cambridge, Massachusetts, 1982.

Kohut, H., Selected Problems of Self Psychological Theory, in *Reflections on Self Psychology,* J. Lichtenberg and S. Kaplan (eds.), Analytic Press, Hillsdale, California, 1978.

Stith-Prothrow, D. and A. Weissman, *Deadly Consequences,* Harper, New York, 1991.

Viorst, J., *Necessary Losses,* Random House, New York, 1986.

CHAPTER 9

Schools and Military Crises

Linda Reed Maxwell

Military children live a unique lifestyle. Like many other children, they can experience divorce in the family, the addition of a sibling, a move to a new home, and developmental changes as they grow up. Each of these changes can be considered a loss. However, military children may face more complicated adjustments in their lives than children who are not being raised by a military parent or guardian. When a military crisis occurs, they will need the support of all of the caring adults (parents, other relatives, teachers, counselors) in their lives.

MILITARY CHILDREN AND LOSS

Military children tend to move on a fairly regular basis. An average military assignment can last from eighteen months to three years. However, shorter and longer assignments occur due to the requirements of the job. With each of these moves, these children are faced with many losses:

- loss of friends,
- loss of home,
- loss of school,
- loss of familiar people (dentists, doctors, neighbors, and baby-sitters), and
- loss of familiar places (schools, library, neighborhood, recreational facilities).

They also must adjust to the loss of routine—the familiarity that goes along with living in one place. Some of these routines may include athletic teams, clubs (Girl Scouts, Boy Scouts, soccer teams), and church activities. Many of these losses can be replaced in a new city, but the loss still occurs. Adjustments must be made. New friends, new homes, and new routines must be found. Along with the loss of routine, the military child must endure the routine absence of a parent. Military lifestyle often calls for the parent or other family member to leave on assignments for periods of time ranging from short periods of a few weeks to longer separations of six months or more.

There are times when no information can be obtained as to the anticipated length of this separation. One of these times is when a war or world crisis occurs. The child not only experiences the absence of the parent, but may also fear for a parent's safety. The extensive media coverage on radio and TV can cause the child to become very concerned about how world events are effecting the parent.

When a war or major crisis occurs, children are often forgotten or ignored, not out of deliberate neglect, but from a lack of understanding. Adults may easily be caught up in their own fears and concerns for a loved one's safety. They may become mesmerized by TV news coverage of the war and the changes it is causing in their own lives. The remaining parent (or guardian) may want to protect children from pain, but *caring adults need to realize that children do hurt even when they do not understand the circumstances in their world*. Children can become confused and afraid regardless of their age when a loved one is involved in any way in a war or world crisis.

It might seem easier to simply ignore the situation. Some may believe that children will adjust on their own. However, damage occurs when major changes and there is no attempt to deal with the associated losses. Ansberry and Hymowitz state that war will inevitably affect children [1]. Kantrowitz and Mason support this stating that military children will have problems when a parent leaves on a war assignment [2].

Claudia L. Jewett writes extensively on childhood losses in her book *Helping Children Cope with Separation and Loss* [3]. She states that the self-esteem of children can be affected when children are not helped. Some children handle the absence of a parent better than others. The age and sex of children play a role in their ability to adjust [4]. Other factors affecting the ability to adjust are family stability, previous experience with separation, and preparation prior to the departure of the parent.

Another reason to help military children during a war crisis centers on the issue of trust. Children who experience parental separation may feel abandoned. They may have trouble trusting the returning parent when the assignment is over. Children who have mothers absent due to a military assignment are at greater risk if the mother is the primary care-giver. If this loss also involves a change of home, there is a higher chance that problems will occur.

HELPLESSNESS

Some children feel responsible for the parent's departure and they believe their behavior or words have caused the parent's absence. This belief can cause children to show signs of helplessness. They may appear discouraged and unable to cope with normal responsibilities. Children may also exhibit the opposite of helplessness by demonstrating a need for excessive control of their environment and the people around them. They may become obsessed with order in their environment and schoolwork. (During the Persian Gulf War, one child continuously straightened her room and anything in her home that seemed "out of order." She stacked magazines, straightened her mother's desk, picked up shoes and put away clothes left on furniture.)

One way to help children who are experiencing helplessness or a greater need for control is to answer questions they may have—both spoken and unspoken. When children do not understand a loss in their lives, they will often fantasize. Some of these fantasies can be worse than the real life situations. Addressing these questions should be done at children's age level of understanding. Questions should always be dealt with honestly, even if the answer is, "I don't know." According to Sofer, this is a good time to use your personal religious beliefs to give answers [5]. Personal faith is for some the only source in which strength and answers can be found.

REACTIONS TO LOSS

Reactions to lifestyle losses and changes can be compared to the reactions experienced by a person who has experienced a death loss. Wolfelt states that a death loss may be the most profound loss that can be experienced, but that other losses—major and minor—will be present during the lives of children [6]. Jewett also supports this view [3]. Children experiencing the loss of a parent due to a war can exhibit many of these reactions. These reactions can be severe because there is usually a short amount of time for preparation, and very few definite answers can be given when children ask questions, such as, ". . . for how long?" The parent may not know how long the assignment will last, what his/her specific duties will be, or how much danger will be present.

Physical symptoms related to the separation may be the most apparent reactions. These symptoms may include: headaches, muscle tension, rashes, lack of energy, change in appetite, nervousness (such as nail-biting or the inability to sit still in class), changes in sleeping patterns, increased allergies, colds, stomach and digestive problems, and/or ear infections. Some children may even experience color blindness because of the excessive stress [7]. Younger children may also revert to an earlier developmental level. This happens because they felt safer during that time. They may thumbsuck, cry, whine, or wet the bed. They may also have a greater need for physical attention, such as rocking and holding. This is a time when the remaining parent or guardian needs to make an effort to give more physical attention—touching, hugging [5]. This can help reduce the stress level of children.

DENIAL

Physical symptoms alone appear to be enough reason to help a child whose parent or guardian may be gone. However, these are not the only loss reactions that can be seen. Many children will experience denial when they learn of a parent's impending departure for a war or crisis assignment. This can manifest itself in many ways. Children may refuse to help the parent prepare to leave, since helping could imply acceptance or even approval of the separation. They may think the parent is on the phone or arriving in a car, instead of acknowledging that they are gone. Hyperactivity may also be a form of denial. Children might talk or move excessively. This continuous physical activity helps them avoid thinking about the pending or current separation. Denial is one of the body's ways of adjusting to a stressful event, but prolonged denial may have negative long-term consequences.

ANGER

The denial phase diminishes as the separation is accepted. However, anger may take its place. Children do not always understand that parents do not have a choice in whether to accept a war-related assignment. They may feel deserted and reject the departing parent. Anger can be shown in fighting, hitting, yelling, or even through "punishment" by non-cooperation and withdrawal. Children need help finding suitable outlets for their anger (such as tearing up newspapers, kicking cardboard boxes, working with modeling clay, or riding a bicycle).

Anger at God is also normal. Children may reject their family's religious beliefs, feeling that God is not taking care of their family. It is important to remain focused on the need of the child to express his/her anger and to not be sidetracked because it is God upon whom they decide to vent it. An attempt to bargain with God may occur as one way of changing the parent's assignment. When the bargaining does not work, anger can be the result. Anger that is unresolved or suppressed can even lead to depression.

DEPRESSION

Children who feel they cannot afford to let their anger show may become depressed. If what they feel is "bad," such as anger, then they will not allow themselves to feel at all. They could have mood swings, aggressive behavior, change in eating habits, or helplessness. There may be an inability to concentrate, or a shortening of the normal attention span and school performance may drop as a result. Children with special needs or learning disabilities are at special risk at this time and any recent progress on their part may seem to be lost. Disorganization in habits and living environment may also manifest itself.

Children can also react to the remaining parent's depression. Children tend to mirror the important adults in their lives. If those adults are coping well, the children will have a better chance of adjusting to the separation. When adults, themselves, are not able to adjust, children will probably have trouble also. It is critical for the remaining parent or guardian to take care of herself/himself and to seek help if that need is present.

FEAR

Fear is another normal reaction to a parent's departure for a war assignment. Normal age-related issues may take second place to worry for a parent's safety. For example, a teenager can easily lose interest in make-up or clothes when there is an overriding concern for a parent who is leaving. Children may also become apprehensive that the remaining parent will leave. If there is a chance of this occurring, children should be told what arrangements have been made for their continued care. There is a possibility that children will want to stay home more. This can be due to regression or to fear that the remaining parent will not be home when school is over. In war, there is also fear that a parent will die, especially if casualties have already occurred. Adults can help by encouraging children to verbalize their fear, and by discussing what could happen. If a child's fear is not dealt with, it will only be buried inside, while the pressure it exerts continues to grow. It will not go away.

GUILT

Guilt is another reaction that needs to be verbalized. The time prior to a separation can be very stressful, and when the separation actually begins, relief is often the result. This is usually short-lived, however, and is replaced by guilt. Children may have said or done things that are regretted after the parent leaves and wish there was a way to undo them, or the guilt may result from having felt "relief" after the departure. Adult help in writing letters or making audio tapes is one way of dealing with this.

ADJUSTMENT AND PREPARATION

Children will normally make some adjustments to a parent's absence. During a war or world crisis, however, many feelings and reactions will not completely go away until the parent returns. There are ways to help children before, during, and after the separation. Before a separation occurs, it is helpful to tell children as much as possible. There is an old saying that, "knowledge is power." In this case, the power comes from giving the child a feeling of some control at a critical point in his/her life. All of this information should be age-appropriate and should be done according to the child's ability to understand. The following steps have been shown to be beneficial:

- Use a map to show where the parent will be. If there is a tentative schedule, place it where the child can see it.
- Explain to the child the job that the parent will do. All people are not involved in combat, and if this is the case, many fears can be avoided.
- It is important for children to know why their parent is leaving. Tell them why the parent's job is important.
- Children can help the parent pack. This allows a special opportunity for special notes to be inserted by the child for the parent to discover later.
- If the parent is leaving on a ship, it may be possible for children to visit the ship, take pictures of the living environment, or see exactly where the parent will be sleeping. Navy personnel are often assigned to a ship and will remain on that ship during a crisis.

- It also helps children if a picture is taken of each child with the departing parent. These pictures can be individually framed and placed in each child's room. Copies can be sent with the parent who is leaving. These pictures help children remember that their relationship to that parent is very important. The importance of these pictures should not be underestimated. It might be wise to use two cameras, (or to have some polaroid photos takes) to be sure that at least one set of prints is available.

INTERVENTIONS AFTER DEPARTURE

Things can also be done to help children after the departure has occurred. It is often a time when children, as well as the remaining parent, feel lost.

- It is critical to keep a schedule, to eat meals as a family. No television should be permitted at meals so that there will be positive interaction. Prolonged viewing of television is often used to mask emotions or even depression.
- Family members should talk together, cry together if they need to and hold each other. It is okay for the remaining parent to show that they hurt also, as this gives children permission to show their pain. Teachers should be prepared for possible displays of emotion in school and to be prepared to support the affected child and his/her classmates.
- Share time with other military families. While it is important to keep routines that were previously established, it is good to add activities that include other families who have a parent (parents) gone. It helps to know there are others who are going through the same thing.
- Spend time as a family writing letters, making treats to send, drawing pictures, making audio tapes.
- Do not be afraid to use humor to cope. Humor is very important. Laughter can be healing. Remember to do things that are fun—riding bikes, playing games, or telling stories.
- Children enjoy stories about their parents, how they met, or the things they did as children. These stories are an important of a family's history and knowing them can give children a sense of continuity and belonging.
- One last important note, include the school in the child's support system. *It is crucial to let school teachers and counselors know that a parent is involved in a war assignment.* There are often

counselor-led support groups for children. These groups are another resource for helping a child realize that he/she is not the only one who has a parent (or other family member) gone on a war assignment. Teachers and counselors can also watch for changes in behavior, grades, or work habits.

For more ideas on how to handle this type of separation, military bases have support centers. Navy support centers are called Family Service Centers. They are on most Navy bases, and can give information about other avenues of help.

FAMILY REUNIONS

Children usually adapt in some ways to a parent's absence. The parent's return, however, does not mean that everything will revert to the pattern the family followed before the parent left. Children whose father has left often become very dependent on the mother [4]. A parent's return may cause resentment and it will take time to adjust to that parent's presence, just as there was a period of adjustment to the absence. The returning parent must move back into the family unit slowly, even though physically, he/she may be home. Young children may not remember the returning parent, and may be hesitant to go to him/her. As with each phase of the separation, time will usually solve many of the adjustment problems that arise. Parents need to be patient as the family comes back together.

War is a critical event in the life of a family. Its impact knows no boundaries and children of military personnel will be effected in all phases of their lives. There are no definites: no time frames to work with, no assurance that a parent will return. Children will react to each phase of a separation, and to the return of the parent. For many children this is a time of crisis, a time when much love and understanding is required of adults who are part of these children's lives. The impact of war can be turned into a time of learning, a time of growth in relationships. It can be a time when children learn much about themselves and their ability to handle future crisis that may enter their lives.

REFERENCES

1. C. Ansberry, and C. Hymowitz, Gulf War Takes a Toll on Soldiers' Children, *Citizen,* Focus on the Family, Pomona, California, 1991.
2. B. Kantrowitz and M. Mason, The Soldier-Parent Dilemma, *Newsweek,* November 12, 1990.

3. C. L. Jewett, *Helping Children Cope with Separation and Loss,* The Harvard Common Press, Cambridge, Massachusetts, 1982.
4. P. L. Adams, J. R. Milner, and N. A. Schrepf, *Fatherless Children,* John Wiley and Sons, New York, 1984.
5. B. Sofer, A Family in Wartime, *Parents,* April 1991.
6. A. Wolfelt, *Death and Grief: A Guide for Clergy,* Accelerated Development, Muncie, Indiana, 1988.
7. M. W. Lefler, Riding Out the (Desert) Storm: Children on the Home Front, *Navy Family Lifeline, 26*:4, 1990.

BIBLIOGRAPHY

Barlow, D., Students and War Stress, *The Education Digest, 56*:8, 1991.

Bernstein, J. E., *Books to Help Children Cope with Separation and Loss,* R. R. Bowker Company, New York, 1983.

Brinkman, D., NavSta San Diego's FSC Offers a Helping Hand, *Navy Family Lifeline, 26*:4, 1990.

Desert Storm in the Classroom, *Education Digest, 57*:1, 1991.

Embry, D. D., *Someone in My Family Went off to the Middle East,* Project ME, Tuscon, Arizona, 1990.

First Aid for Kids' Fears about War, *Newsweek, 117*:66, 1991.

First Baptist Church of Norfolk, *What Kids and Families Can Do When Dad is Helping His Country and Away from Home,* First Baptist Church of Norfolk, Norfolk, Virginia, 1991.

Gelman, D., When Little Children Have Big Worries, *Newsweek, 117*, 1991.

Grisoli, C., DoD Responds to Family Member Concerns, *Navy Family Lifeline, 26*:4, 1990.

Huang, T., Images of War and Peace, *The Virginia Pilot* (newspaper), Norfolk, Virginia, February 17, 1991.

Kerr, M., *What Kids and Families Can Do When Dad is in the Navy and Going out to Sea,* Thoroughgood Elementary School, Virginia Beach, Virginia, 1988.

Lackey, P. K., Navy Doctor Stresses Consistency with Child when Parent is at War, *Virginia Pilot* (newspaper), Norfolk, Virginia, February 17, 1991.

Navy Family Services Center, *Families and Deployment,* Little Creek Naval Amphibious Base Family Service Center, Norfolk, Virginia, 1990.

Sanders, A. L., When Dad and Mom Go to War, *Time, 137*:69, 1991.

Silver, M., Helping Children Confront the War, *U.S. News and World Report, 110*:65, 1991.

Virginia Beach City Public Schools, Desert Storm: School Counselors Provide Reassurance, *Insight,* Virginia Beach City Public Schools, Virginia Beach, Virginia, March 1991.

What Parents Need to Say, *Newsweek, 117,* 1991.

Wolfelt, A., Helping Children Cope with Grief, *Accelerated Development,* Muncie, Indiana, 1983.

CHAPTER 10

Support Groups in the Schools

Sandra Elder

INTRODUCTION

On their own, children and adolescents often lack the resources, cognitive ability and experience to deal effectively with a significant loss. Without help, they may fail to thrive following the losses which are certain to happen in their lives and will be affected to an even greater degree by the multiple losses which typically accompany and follow a crisis. Conversely, with help, these same children can build and grow from their experiences.

For the sake of our children, we take responsibility for empowerment. This empowerment is intended to foster lives that unfold rather than contract, lives that connect to life rather than separate from it. Adults are transmitters of life to children. As we take responsibility for this role, we can seek to provide these children with the knowledge that *pain often has gain*. Through "loss remembered" they can become co-creators in a life that provides for growth and meaning and restores unity and peace.

Grief is a human process to be experienced. It is NOT an illness to be treated. It is as important to learn to grieve as it is to learn arithmetic, language or science. Children witness and feel changes in their lives, often without the skills to express their fears and pain. Grief is a *life skill* to be learned and lived.

Western culture often fails to support the very process which helps people to recover from the pain of sadness and loss . . . GRIEF! Because they lack both control and competency, children experiencing loss and death are more at risk than adults. Children experience the pain of loss without having mastered attitudes and skills to help them cope with that pain.

It has been established that the *intensity* and *duration* of stress resulting from the adverse circumstances of loss can be decreased. This can be accomplished through:

- mastery of coping skills,
- support,
- attitudes which accompany feelings of hope, and
- the knowledge that the experiences of grief are *normal* [1, pp. 3, 4, 6, 41].

The "good news" is that, to reach these goals, concerned educators need not reinvent the wheel. There are many existing programs which seek to develop the points mentioned above through education and support. One of the most popular vehicles for education and support is the school-based support group.

HOW SUPPORT GROUPS ASSIST STUDENTS

What is it like to be a bereaved adolescent? What are the tasks which bereaved children and adolescents need to accomplish? How can programs offering mutual aid and self help assist bereaved adolescents? Charles Corr, speaking to the World Gathering on Bereavement, held in Seattle, Washington, offered the following suggestions:

- Demonstrate to young people that they need not be alone or marked out in a pejorative sense. They may be in a different or unusual situation compared to many of their peers, but there are other adolescents who are also bereaved. This requires deep respect for the individual and his/her autonomy.
- Providing information about, and frameworks for, making sense of both death-related experiences and experiences of grief and mourning. An adolescent must determine the significance of a crisis, just at the time in which he/she is taking control of and claiming and shaping his or her own life.
- Help to identify, validate, and normalize strong feelings and other unusual experiences which are associated with loss, grief, and mourning.
- Provide permission and a safe place in which to confront and express those feelings.

- Emphasize the positive legacy that endures from a lost relationship with a loved one or thing, and by suggesting constructive ways in which to remember or memorialize life that is now ended.
- Demonstrate in non-judgmental ways the conviction or trust that life and living can and do go on, by providing mentors and temporary role models, and acting out options or different ways in which individuals find "new normals" in their lives.

For adolescents and some children this is likely to relate especially to pressures involving changed roles and to identity formation. Support groups attest to the fact that those who have been grievously wounded can find ways to go forward and can even help each other. This is re-empowerment at its best [2].

THE NEEDS OF GRIEVING ADOLESCENTS

Alan Wolfelt has long worked with bereaved adolescents and has identified six basic needs which they share. He states that these adolescents need to:

- experience and express outside of themselves the reality of the death,
- encounter the pain of the loss while being nurtured physically, emotionally, and spiritually,
- learn to convert the relationship with the person who has died from one of interactive presence to one of *appropriate* memory,
- develop a new self-identity based on a life without the person who has died,
- relate the experience of the death to a context of meaning,
- experience a continued supportive and stabilizing adult presence after the loss and in future years [3].

DEVELOPING A NEW SELF-IDENTITY

The death of a loved one loved can permanently change a child's self-image. The specific roles the person who died played in the child's life are critical parts of a child's self-definition. As children work on this central need of mourning, every aspect of their capacity to cope is tested. The bereaved child often thinks, feels and acts in ways that previously may have seemed totally unlike him or herself. This process appears to be an inherent part of the search for a new identity in the absence of the person who has died. Social and functional role changes also must be integrated into the bereaved child's reality, they typically become a vital part of the child's self-concept.

Beyond the change in self-identity, the death of someone in the family also requires people, children included, to take on new roles that had been filled by the person who died. It is a part of the "normal" process of bereavement that a grieving person may take on some of the traits or behaviors of the deceased. When a child exhibits behaviors linked to a deceased older person, well-intended, yet misinformed, adults (including teachers) sometimes reinforce a new "hypermature" identity on the part of the bereaved child. While everyone in the family will have new roles and responsibilities when a death occurs, we should never assign inappropriate role responsibilities to children. To encourage a child to be a "man" or "woman" for their family, or for the sake of the person who died, can damage the child's capacity to do the work of mourning.

As caring adults, we have a responsibility to "walk with" bereaved children as they struggle with many of these self-identity issues. A desire to understand, a capacity to listen and learn and provide consistency, an environment which nurtures trust and security in the child during this time is critically important [3]. The school, where children and adolescents spend the greatest part of each weekday, has a special obligation to find a way to provide for these needs. Support groups in the school offer one way of meeting these needs. The Living and Learning Through Loss Program is presented here as a detailed model which was employed by a school system to aid bereaved students who were dealing with personal losses.

LIVING AND LEARNING THROUGH LOSS: A PROGRAM OF THE SHORELINE COMMUNITY SCHOOL ASSOCIATION–VICTORIA, BRITISH COLUMBIA

Many adolescents in our society experience the personal crisis of a loss of at least one significant relationship. This loss can occur as a result of unresolved family breakdown, transient households or the death or serious illness of a family member or close friend. The tragedy of loss adds to the normal turbulence of adolescence and may lead to an increased incidence of stress-related problems and behaviors such as substance abuse, destructive sexual behavior, suicide, crime, premature departure from school or home, or psychosomatic disorders.

Adolescents experiencing loss need to be supported as they look openly and honestly at themselves and the relationship that has been lost or radically altered. *Skilled* support needs to be directed at helping these young people begin a process of healing which, in turn, will lead to a willingness to invest in future significant relationships.

The Living and Learning Through Loss Program is sponsored by the Shoreline Community School Association. It provides an opportunity for "at risk" adolescents to explore their responses to situations of loss in a supportive group environment. The intent of the program is to provide participants with positive coping skills for dealing with loss before maladaptive behaviors become entrenched, and to prepare participants to deal with future losses in a productive and healthy way.

MAGNITUDE OF THE PROBLEM

In Greater Victoria, an average of six adolescent suicide attempts are reported per month. According to the Canadian Mental Health Association the most common precursors of suicide and suicide attempts are stress factors, such as the loss of a loved one through death or the breakup of a relationship. Suicide can be an extreme manifestation of unresolved grief. Alcohol and drug abuse, vandalism, "runaways" and "drop outs" can also be linked to situations of relationship loss.

In January 1988, the Student Services Team at Shoreline Community School identified twenty students out of a population of 400 who, within the previous six months, had experienced the loss of a significant relationship as a result of a death. The number of losses due to unresolved family breakdown and household transience was far greater.

One might reasonably ask why this was not simply handled through referral to local mental health services. In fact, few adolescent mental health services exist in the Greater Victoria area. Resources that do exist are over extended. Mental Health Centers have waiting lists of at least three months and psychiatrists specializing in work with adolescents have waiting lists of three to six months. Treatment interventions are available only after the young person has demonstrated *severe* "at risk" or maladaptive behaviors.

The Living and Learning Through Loss Program addresses a serious gap by providing a much needed preventive resource for these "at risk" adolescents. To date, the program has provided these services to approximately 200 young adults in Greater Victoria and surrounding areas. The number of participants in each group has increased significantly since its inception and this number includes both female and young adult male participants.

PURPOSE

The purpose of the Living and Learning Through Loss Program is to provide a series of peer support group programs. These programs are aimed at helping adolescents develop positive coping skills and behaviors for dealing with the grief associated with the loss of a significant relationship. It is anticipated that group participants will develop a more positive attitude and approach to life.

TARGET POPULATION

The program is designed for adolescents between the ages of twelve and nineteen years old who have experienced the loss of a significant relationship through death, terminal illness, family breakdown or family transiency.

OBJECTIVES

Program Objectives

The Living and Learning Through Loss program has four main objectives. It seeks to:

1. Create an open and supportive group environment that promotes the sharing of information, ideas and feelings regarding the issues of death and loss.
2. Develop an understanding, awareness and acceptance of normal grief reactions.
3. Identify and enhance specific coping skills and behaviors in dealing with death and loss situations.
4. Develop a more positive attitude and approach to everyday living.

Learning Objectives

Learning objectives of the program seek to assist grieving adolescents to:

1. *Accept the reality of their losses.*
   The grieving adolescents are allowed to express feelings and thoughts related to their loss(es). Denial is a frequent barrier to completing this task and may involve denial of the facts of the loss, the meaning of the loss, or the irreversibility of the loss.
2. *Be willing to experience the pain of the grief process and to understand and know that grieving is normal and expected.* Since grieving is an *active* process, grieving adolescents need to face

and relive the pain of the loss. They need to grieve the good, as well as the bad sides of the past relationship because this can help them to acknowledge and begin to deal with unhappiness, anger, frustration, and weakness. As the pain is relived and feelings released, the slow process of healing begins [4].

3. *Make the necessary adjustments in their environment and to provide emotional support.*
   Group members deal with problem-solving skills and ways of coping with the altered state of their family and the new relationships that have developed as a result of these losses.
4. *To redirect their emotional energy away from their lost relationships and to invest in new relationships.*
   This involves helping grieving adolescents to see that their losses can never be regained, providing them with additional resources, and helping them in the formation of new relationships.

REFERRAL SOURCES

The primary source of referrals of group members are teachers and counselors from the three school districts of Sooke, Saanich and Greater Victoria. Referrals are also received and accepted from physicians, parents, Hospice Victoria, private counselors, other youth-service agencies, and peers (most often, adolescents who have participated in this program).

SCREENING/INTAKE PROCESS

Following the referral, each adolescent is interviewed by the facilitator of the program and is provided with detailed information about the format and expectations of the program. The only requirements of the participants in this program are that it is the adolescent's decision to participate in this program, that confidentiality is assured and that he/she will attend *every* group session.

The screening interview provides an opportunity for the facilitator to gain a better understanding of the individual needs of the group members. In addition, participants are introduced to the group facilitator by the program facilitator. This decreases the anxiety often associated with the initial group session.

GROUP PROCESS

The Living and Learning Through Loss Program consists of eight weekly group sessions of two hours duration. Group attendance is limited to eight to ten participants. The group sessions are held at a meeting place that is centrally located. Sometimes having the meeting place in the school or a nearby church may have a negative impact on the comfort of the participants. The group sessions are primarily offered during the evening hours at a time that suits the needs of the participants. Adolescents tend to have numerous after school demands, i.e., jobs, responsibilities at home or time with peers. These should be considered in selecting the day and time to meet.

The groups provide a vehicle for counseling and peer support that is both knowledge and experience based. The peer support helps to counteract the tendency of some adolescents to isolate themselves from their support systems when they are grieving a loss. Although designed to offer support in a group environment, provision is made for one-to-one counseling where necessary to help an individual function more effectively in the group.

As part of the process, group sessions utilize poems, music, art therapy techniques, selected reading material used in an approach known as bibliotherapy, video presentations, movies, cartoons, and information about grief of loss issues.

OVERVIEW OF THE WEEKLY GROUP SESSIONS
SESSION 1: INTRODUCTION

PROGRAM OBJECTIVE: to create an open and supportive group environment that promotes the sharing of information, ideas and feelings regarding issues of death and loss.

LEARNING OBJECTIVE: Participants should become better able to accept the reality of their losses.

IMPLEMENTATION STRATEGY:

1. The facilitator provides an overview of the eight week program emphasizing the program objectives and learning objectives.
2. Participants introduce themselves by stating their names, schools, grades and they state why they are attending the program.
3. Hopes and Fears Exercise: The purpose of this exercise is to diffuse apprehensions that participants may have about being in the group and to help participants realize that other adolescents have similar thoughts, feelings and behaviors,

   OR

   A video presentation of five adolescents sharing their grief and losses on a public television program. The adolescents in this video all participated in the Living and Learning Through Loss Program and shared those experiences with the television audience.

4. Group Rules: The group rules are few but are essential to the group process. They are:
   - regular attendance—this is NOT a drop-in group,
   - confidentiality of information shared within the group,
   - that participation is *voluntary* for the participants,
   - participants have permission to pass when unable or unwilling to contribute during the group sharing or activities.

SESSION 2: IDENTIFICATION OF LOSSES AND ASSOCIATED THOUGHTS, FEELINGS, AND BEHAVIORS

PROGRAM OBJECTIVE: to create an open and supportive group environment that promotes the sharing of information, ideas, and feelings regarding issues of death and loss.

LEARNING OBJECTIVE: Participants will learn to accept the reality of their losses.

IMPLEMENTATION STRATEGY:

1. Participants complete an inventory of the losses that they have experienced during adolescence, The Adolescent Life Change Event Scale [5].
2. Participants complete a list of their thoughts, feelings and behaviors associated with each loss-related event in their lives (or as many as they can).

SESSION 3: EXPRESSING GRIEF REACTIONS

PROGRAM OBJECTIVE: To develop an understanding, awareness and acceptance of normal grief reactions.

LEARNING OBJECTIVE: To assist participants to be willing to experience the pain of the grief process and to understand that grieving is normal and expected.

IMPLEMENTATION STRATEGY:

1. Art Therapy Technique: Seven feelings are listed: happy, sad, anger, love, fear, pain, and separation. Participants are asked to identify the colors and symbols associated with each of these seven feelings and to identify the people, places, things and events in their lives with which each of the seven feelings is linked [6].

SESSION 4: UNDERSTANDING GRIEF AND LOSS

PROGRAM OBJECTIVE: To develop an understanding, awareness and acceptance of normal grief reactions.

LEARNING OBJECTIVE: To assist participants to be willing to experience the pain of the grief process and to understand that grieving is normal and expected.

IMPLEMENTATION STRATEGY:

1. "Family Ties" Video Presentation: This video chronicles Alex Keaton's grief reactions to the death of a friend. This video serves as a catalyst for a discussion of normal grief and loss reactions. Participants are encouraged to identify with Alex and to compare his grief reactions to their own.

SESSION 5: COPING WITH GRIEF AND LOSS (A)

PROGRAM OBJECTIVE: To identify and enhance specific coping skills and behaviors in dealing with death and loss situations.

LEARNING OBJECTIVE: Participants will begin to adjust to the new environment created by their losses, and to provide support to one another.

IMPLEMENTATION STRATEGY:

1. The Four Quadrants of Wellness: Participants are introduced to four fundamental needs that must be balanced for a healthy lifestyle—physical, emotional, intellectual, and spiritual.
2. Video Presentation: "Suicide and Depression" by Michael Pritchard. This video presentation explores the ways in which adolescents can learn to deal appropriately with feelings of depression and thoughts of suicide.
3. The Grief Model ["Figure 8"]: This model helps participants to visualize their internal thoughts and feelings and the external behaviors associated with normal grief (see Figure 1).

SESSION 6: COPING WITH GRIEF AND LOSS (B)

PROGRAM OBJECTIVE: To identify and enhance specific coping skills and behaviors in dealing with death and loss situations.

LEARNING OBJECTIVE: Participants will begin to adjust to the new environment created by their losses, and to provide support to one another.

IMPLEMENTATION STRATEGY:

1. Participants brainstorm the specific coping skills that they can use in dealing with situations related to loss. The list of coping skills becomes a basis for identifying skills which are healthy and those which are unhealthy.
2. Grief Reactions: Participants are encouraged to share the music, art, poetry, etc., that best expresses their reactions to grief and loss.

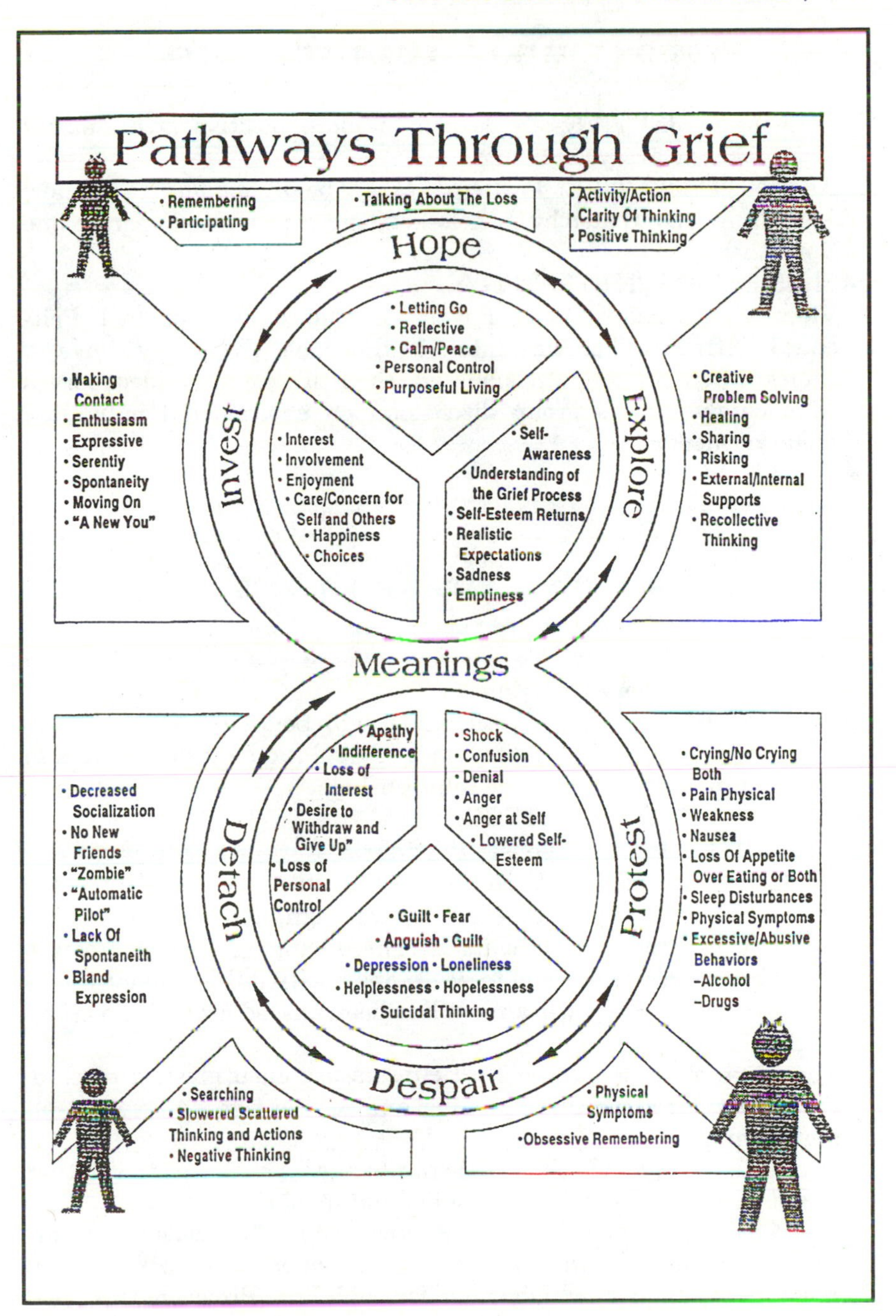

Figure 1. Pathways through grief.
Source: Lamers (1978), Martin and Elder (1988).

SESSION 7: MAKING POSITIVE CHOICES

PROGRAM OBJECTIVE: To develop a more positive attitude and approach to everyday living.

LEARNING OBJECTIVE: Participants will begin to adjust to the new environment created by their losses, and to provide support to one another.

IMPLEMENTATION STRATEGY:

1. Video Presentation: "The Power of Choice" by Michael Pritchard introduces participants to the idea that they have a choice when making decisions in their lives. The video serves as a catalyst for a group discussion on choices and individual empowerment.

SESSION 8: LIFE AFTER LOSS

PROGRAM OBJECTIVE: To develop a more positive attitude and approach to everyday living.

LEARNING OBJECTIVE: Participants will begin to redirect their emotional energy away from their lost relationships/losses and to invest in new more positive relationships.

IMPLEMENTATION STRATEGY:

1. The "I AM" Closing Exercise: Participants are asked to write one positive thing about each group member on a sheet of paper that has each participants name at the top right hand corner of the paper. These written comments are shared among the participants. Participants are also asked to write one positive thing about themselves on their own paper after it has been passed around the group circle.
2. The Piece of Rose Quartz: Participants are each given a piece of rose quartz as a symbol of healing and the capacity to love oneself and others.
3. Evaluation and Feedback: Participants have a choice as to whether or not they put the names on the evaluation sheet.
4. The Celebration of Life Meal: Participants will decide on a restaurant of their choice (group decision) where they will share a meal. In the Living and Learning Through Loss Program, this meal is paid for by an anonymous donor whose grief process is related to the death of his young son and has another child with a life-threatening illness.

PROGRAM EVALUATION

The Living and Learning Through Loss Program has been evaluated by an outside group, the British Columbia Health Care Research Foundation. This group identified a number of weaknesses and strengths in the program which are offered here in a shortened form in the belief that they may be useful to others seeking to start support groups.

Identified Weaknesses

1. *Lack of Distinctions:*

There have been no significant differences identified in the manner in which the programs responds to the losses of bereavement and the losses of divorce. The salience of their commonalities do not outweigh the impact of their differences. One will never again see in the flesh a person who has died! The anger of the bereaved often has guilt as a constant companion. This intensity of anger and guilt is not always a feature of the anger at divorced parents. One cannot ever compensate or console the dead parent or sibling for behavior towards them when alive. It is not unusual for every member of a bereaved family to be silent, isolated from each other in their grief so that no one knows what the others think and feel.

There is no distinction among different types of death, that is, suicide, sudden, violent, lingering, etc. Grieving includes *universals* of emotions, thoughts, behaviors, however, there are *specifics* of timing, guilt, anger, fantasies, duration and effects upon one's life. The loss of a beloved grandparent may indeed be sad to a grandchild, but "expected" in the order of things. The loss of a sibling has major consequences for both the family's structure and future, and for the adolescent's developing personality. Death by suicide leaves a legacy of rage unequaled in all other deaths.

Intensely bereaved people are expected to "get over it" (usually meaning, become normal again!) and shortly after the funeral to disguise their sorrows while in public. To survive as a social being connected to their social networks, a common disguise of their sorrow is to act "as if" they were "over it." In contrast, children of divorce, although suffering from the breakdown of their families, because of the large numbers of peers in their situation, are sanctioned to engage openly in grieving and emoting.

2. *No Breakdown of Age Groupings*

There are different developmental stages in the years we assign to the period of adolescence, each one requiring different mental, emotional, and behavioral tasks. Outcome results may not be as positive as they could be if this age/stage variable were identified and accounted for in the program's intervention menu.

3. *Time Elapsed Since the Loss*

As the grieving process may not even begin for several months or years after the death of a parent or sibling, it is the belief of the reviewers that participation in a group may have no relevance or rationale to a student who has contracted for membership because of his bereavement circumstances. Some members, then, may receive no benefits from the experience and assume they are inadequate, deficient, etc. Such a false assessment of self-blame does nothing to relieve the inevitable lowered self-esteem of the griever.

It is alright to mix short and long durations of bereavement in one group. But not to mention the dimension of "elapsed time" may render some intervention strategies irrelevant to some members. Positive outcome results may be impaired as a whole by this one important, overlooked variable.

4. *The Relationship of the Adolescent to the Deceased*

At the death of a parent, children, usually lose two parents as the surviving parent may, in fact, not be capable of further parenting while in the throws of his or her own grief. When a child has died, both parents are often unable to nurture the other children. This lack of ability to continue nurturing is certainly present in spouses during the separation and divorce process but, in the opinion of the reviewers, it is not equal in intensity and recovery time to bereaved parents.

5. *Unattainable Goals*

The Goal of "Helping Adolescents to Perceive Changes in a More Positive Way . . .": When a parent or sibling dies, any intervention aimed at redefining the death-related changes as "positive" is bound to lose credibility and perhaps engender hostility. For a very long time, there will be nothing positive after the death of a parent or sibling. A more human, less ambitious, and achievable goal would be to "help adolescents perceive there are options when assuming attitudes, behaviors and emotions in response to their changing circumstances."

The statement ". . . helping adolescents . . . learn(ing) how to deal with future changes in their lives": This appears to be a grandiose ambition as it is too general and implies a simplistic, one-dimensional orientation to changes throughout one's lifetime. A more achievable goal could be "to help students gain confidence by facing . . . not hiding from . . . some painful aspect of their present loss situation." One hopes that the adolescent will generalize these newly learned skills to cope with future unplanned and unpleasant changes.

6. *Future Difficulties are Not Mentioned*

There is no reference to the oscillations of thoughts and feelings involved in loss and/or the grief process, or the evolution of grief throughout one's life. The four categories and eight sessions cannot settle, once and for all, the multiple issues related to loss and grief. This needs to be made clear to the participants.

No definition is offered for "reality" in the goal of "accepting the reality of death." In order to prevent the conceptual emptiness of the "reality" trap, the four general goals of griefwork (learning objectives) should be redefined by stating concrete specific, desired behaviors attached to each of these four "learning objectives."

7. *Leadership Training Program*

The content of this teaching program needs to be stated. Effective leadership is a vital part of the success of these groups.

8. *Follow-up Methods*

There needs to be some form of follow-up for the participants in these groups. When adolescents have had significant losses in their lives, there may be many additional crisis events after the groups have concluded their eight sessions. A follow-up for "at risk" adolescents demonstrates to them that somebody does care about them and that they are less likely to feel cut off from a support and nurturing group when it concludes [7].

The schools attended by group participants could serve as the vehicle for such follow-up which could become a part of on-going school-based support for the support group.

Identified Strengths

1. *Positive Coping Skills:* There is an emphasis upon teaching "positive coping skills" before less functional ones are adopted.

2. *Preparation to Address Future Losses:* The preparation to address future losses in productive and healthy ways using this learning experience as a model is clearly a strength.
3. *Investment In Future Relationships:* The option for adolescents to adopt a "healing" model may encourage their investment in future, significant relationships.
4. *Emphasis on Sharing and Connectedness*: An emphasis upon "sharing and connectedness" can assist grieving adolescents to counter feelings of isolation, loneliness, and alienation.
5. *Validation and Communication:* The program gives adolescents the opportunity and sanction to talk of their experiences, and to think through difficulties rather than employing the mechanisms of denial or impulsive behavior.
6. *Peer Helpers:* The perpetuation of this program through recruiting and educating peers as counsellors and helpers is a positive feature.
7. *Initial Screening:* The use of an initial, screening interview allows a group member and a leader to become acquainted with each other and to be clear about the function, goals and desired outcomes of this experience.
8. *Community Involvement:* The involvement of community agencies in providing group leaders and the projected involvement of the lay community for parent support groups are seen as positive features.
9. *Innovation:* This program is very innovative, unique and introduces the presentation and activation of coping skills as an integral part of the weekly sessions.
10. *School-based Applicability:* This program could easily be used in *any* school system, with modifications for local circumstances and personnel. There is nothing in its design or implementation that is limited to a particular local [7].

Due to the demand from adolescents and the community at large, direct service has become the priority of this program. For this reason, we have been unable to conduct an adequate evaluation of this program. Our only basis for evaluation over the past four years has been through the use of direct feedback from the participants themselves (verbal or written) or, on a minimal basis, both verbal and written feedback from the referral sources, that is, parents, doctors, teachers, counselors, other adolescents, mental health agencies, and hospice.

A graduate student from the University of Victoria, Faculty of Education, Department of Psychological Foundations, will be conducting a research project that involves the evaluation of the Living and Learning Through Loss Program. It is hoped that this research project will provide a clearer picture of the ways in which adolescents judge the ability of this program to assist them in their grief process. This evaluation has the potential to assist the program's efforts to secure a solid basis of funding resources for future groups.

The strengths and weaknesses in this program outlined previously were the result of three anonymous evaluators of our proposal for funding through the B.C. Health Care Research Foundation—Health Promotion Grant in 1990. A final comment that was made by one of the anonymous evaluators will be the concluding comment about the program:

> There are many praiseworthy features of this proposal, among them the dynamic of health versus health care; the interrelationship of individuals and the community to health; the promotion of healthy coping skills, preventing harm to the community by forestalling negative coping strategies; connectedness; sharing; and peer support. Last, but not least, this program offers some form of public ritual to express the universal pain of bereavement [7].

OTHER MODELS OF SUPPORT GROUPS FOR BEREAVED STUDENTS

Support groups for young people facing crises, such as personal bereavement or life threatening illness, exist in *many* formats. It is not a bad idea for teachers, counselors, parents, and other caring adults to view with suspicion any program which presents itself as the *only* way of helping bereaved students. The following group models, some of which have accompanying manuals, have shown positive results in the young people they serve.

Adolescents and Death: Bereavement Support Groups for Secondary School Students–Lorne Park Secondary School, Mississauga, Ontario

This program is based on the belief that, in dealing with grief, communication is the key. This communication should take place among students, teachers, parents, and the community as a whole. The program takes place during school hours because:

- Grieving students find school difficult due to a diminished ability to concentrate and remember.
- The group's importance is demonstrated when it becomes a natural part of the school day.

- Students, like teachers, have after-school commitments, such as jobs, lessons, or sporting events.
- Transportation—not all students have access to a car and may have no way of getting to an after-school group meeting.
- It is critical that the adolescent be allowed to grieve and to recognize that some of his or her own peers are facing the same problems.
- The grief process may be emotionally overwhelming for adolescents. At some time after the death, 80 percent of the students said they had considered suicide.
- *All* students have experienced increased home difficulties.

Group Support for Home Difficulties

Adolescents in the support group said that home difficulties developed because more responsibilities were expected by parents. Students felt confused by rule changes. More restrictive rules were imposed or young people suddenly found that there were no rules at all. They were upset at the introduction of a "new" partner for a surviving parent soon after the death of a parent. Suddenly there could be new stepsisters or brothers invading the space of the surviving adolescent(s) and personality clashes between the old and the new family members. A death sometimes necessitated moving to a new home, coupled with a reduction of finances, and the loss of friends, schools, neighbors and pets. The adolescent's health and physical well-being is often affected by sleep disturbances and changes in eating patterns.

Since so much of what is discussed in group deals with home issues, it may be helpful (with the students permission) for these concerns to be shared with the parents. This can improve communication in the home with the remaining parent(s).

Peer counseling has been very helpful within the support group. Students who have participated in a bereavement support group will often volunteer to help other students who are grieving a significant loss. Some students do not want to be part of a support group but still need some support. Often, an older student will "adopt" a younger member of the support group, take the role of big sister or brother and provide peer support. This peer support system, if it already exists, can be most helpful in times of crisis.

It is important to have two leaders in the group for all sessions. Because of the emotional drain around this type of counseling it is important for the leaders to also have support. Training in bereavement counseling is important for anyone considered as a group leader.

Group composition is also very important. Ages and sexes mix well from grades nine to thirteen. However, it is important to have some individuals not in the same group if their problems differ too greatly. For example, immediate family members and boyfriend or girlfriend deaths might be in one group, while those coping with the death of grandparents not living in the home are placed in another group.

Current research indicated without question that those students who are given the opportunity of participating in a group benefit from the experience and are able to lead productive lives sooner than those students who are not able to participate in a group.

When Children Grieve: A Children's Support Group–Prince George Hospice Society

This is an eight week program that combines play and art in a safe, group environment to help children learn about themselves and about the grieving process. It is designed for children ages five years to twelve years of age. Attendance at all sessions is important. The parent is the primary source of emotional support and direction for a child. This program is intended to support the family, not replace it.

Young Person's Grief Support Program: St. Mary's Grief Support Center–Duluth, Minnesota

This program is conducted on three age/developmental levels: five to eight years old, nine to thirteen years old, and fourteen to seventeen years old. It is based at St. Mary's Medical Center and works on an outreach basis.

The Dougy Center: Supporting Children in Grief–Portland, Oregon

This center offers support for grieving children and for those who are a part of their lives. The Dougy Center was established as a tribute to a boy who knew about suffering and fear and realized with the rare insight of a child that both could be met with love, understanding and the joy of life. Doug died at age nine of an inoperable brain tumor. This center makes real the belief that pain often has gain.

CanTeen–New South Wales, Australia.

The CanTeen network offers support for teenagers living with cancer or other life-threatening blood disorders, and for their brothers and sisters. It was begun in Sydney in 1985 and now has branches throughout Australia. Adolescence is a time of life that is normally associated with having fun, taking risks and trying new things as "one of the gang." Cancer has the potential to destroy this way of life. The CanTeen network offers support to maintain a life as close to "normal" as possible for all concerned.

CONCLUSION

There are emotional needs present in young people which have a strong effect on the learning process. In the best of times, a school may not be able to address these needs in each of their students through traditional classroom or counseling services. A crisis in the school can further aggravate this shortcoming. Support groups can be a valuable resource for affected students and for schools. These groups may be based in an individual school or in the community to assist students from several schools. No one model can ever be adequate in addressing the many situations which may arise or the many variables present in a given community. However, the benefits reported by participants in such groups require, at the very least, that a steering committee consider a role for such groups as part of an overall crisis response plan. The ideal time for such an examination is in advance of need, rather than at the moment of crisis, so that there is adequate time for evaluation, recommendation, planning, and implementation.

REFERENCES

1. D. O'Toole, *Growing Through Grief: A K-12 Curriculum to Help Young People Through All Kinds of Loss,* Rainbow Connection, Burnsville, North Carolina, 1989.
2. C. Corr, *Alone Together: Bereaved Adolescents, Mutual Aid and Self-help,* presentation at the World Gathering on Bereavement, Seattle, Washington, August 8, 1991.
3. A. Wolfelt, The Needs and Tasks of Grieving Adolescents, *Bereavement Magazine,* pp. 38-40, June 1991.
4. B. Anschuetz, Ed.D., *A Bereavement Counseling Group For Adolescents: A Training Manual,* B. Anschuetz, Queensville, Ontario, 1990.
5. Yeaworth et al., The Development of an Adolescent Life Change Event Scale, *Adolescence, 15*:57, pp. 91-97, 1980.
6. S. Mai, Mai *Color Glossary: Art Therapy Assessment Technique,* Ottawa, Ontario, 1987.
7. British Columbia Health Care Research Foundation, Health Promotion Grant of the Evaluation Subcommittee, (typewritten), Fall 1990.

BIBLIOGRAPHY

Cunningham, L., *Teen Age Grief (TAG): A Training Manual for Initiating and Facilitating Grief Support Groups for Teens*, Teen Age Grief, Inc., Panama City, California, 1990.

Dorpat, T. L., Suicide, Loss and Mourning, in *Life Threatening Behavior, 3*, pp. 213-224, 1973.

Elder, S. and Martin, K., Pathways through Grief: A Model of the Process, in *Personal Care in an Impersonal World*, J. Morgan (ed.), Baywood, Amityville, New York, 1993.

Reynolds, S. E., *Endings To Beginnings: A Grief Support Group for Children and Adolescents*, HRG Press, Minneapolis, Minnesota, 1992.

Worden, J. W., *Grief Counseling and Grief Therapy: A Handbook for the Mental Health Practitioner*, New York, Springer, 1982.

CHAPTER 11

Critical Incident Stress Debriefing Teams and Schools

Rick Ritter

Critical Incident Stress Debriefing Teams have been developed as a result of the work that has taken place over the last fourteen years in helping individuals to cope more effectively with the stress that accompanies a *critical incident*. A critical incident is an event, or series of events, that creates an exceptionally strong emotional and mental response in those individuals who are affected either directly or indirectly. It has been found that those individuals, or groups of individuals, will possibly experience a certain level of dysfunction in their lives. This dysfunction may occur immediately, or at a later date. There is evidence that certain events can be so stressful that they can overwhelm the capacity for coping, even in healthy individuals. Because this situation has become so widespread, there has been a proliferation of models and theories addressing prevention, intervention, and postvention aspects of these traumatic events. In this case, the word *traumatic* is limited to those events which, when they occur, are considered to be outside of the realm of "normal" human experience. In a school setting we have seen examples of such extraordinary events in the collapse of a school wall on elementary school children during a freak wind storm in New York State, the group suicide of four teens in New Jersey, and growing numbers of student homicides both in and out of school.

Approximately fourteen years ago, based in large part on the work of community-based organizations (C.B.O.s) working with Viet Nam veterans in the United States, Canada and Australia, work was begun to develop effective models for prevention, intervention and postvention efforts as they pertain to the aftermath of traumatic events. This process of exploring for, experimenting with and refining models continues today. As an outgrowth of this effort, there has been specific work in developing field models for aiding emergency service personnel who are traumatized on the job. Emergency service personnel have been defined as fire, police, emergency medicine, mortuary, coroner, and other ancillary personnel. The team of specialists who provide this special service is referred to as a Critical Incident Stress Debriefing (CISD) Team.

THE CRITICAL INCIDENT STRESS DEBRIEFING TEAM

The CISD team is made up of those same varieties of emergency service personnel, joined by mental health professionals from that same locale, who have all completed specialized training. These groups work together as a coordinated unit and offer services to the community, usually on an unpaid, volunteer basis. The individual CISD team members are trained to accomplish the following tasks:

- *Work on/near the scene*: CISD team members, as a group or singly, go to the scene if the incident occurs over an extended period of time or is so severe as to require immediate attention.
- *Assist with demobilization*: Often, when a unit is being stood down, it can be beneficial for individuals to have an opportunity to decompress from a particular incident.
- *Begin initial defusing*: There are many situations where one or more individuals are targeted as having been heavily impacted by an event.
- *Conduct formal debriefings*: The CISD team organizes and manages a formal process in which affected individuals can externalize bothersome thoughts and feelings in order to gain a better perspective on an incident. Others participate to support their colleagues.
- *Provide follow-up services*: The mental health personnel monitor the situation, with a central contact person, in the days and weeks that follow to review just how well affected individuals are coping.
- *Offer individual consultation*: It is recommended that such consultations be offered. Referrals can be made if requested or if it appears that such referral is appropriate.

CISD teams are scattered across the country and each year many people receive basic or advanced training in order to establish new teams or to add to the personnel available to existing teams.

THE CISD TEAM AND THE SCHOOL

CISD teams are a potential resource available to schools in their communities. The task for each school is to establish a working relationship with these teams (the team name and purpose may differ from one region to another) and with similar community resources. In the past, there has been a tendency on the part of schools to wait until there is a problem. Something is then thrown together and we hope that it will be sufficient to deal with the crisis. We owe our children and all members of the school community a better proposition than that. In addition to the CISD team, there are other resources which can be made available to the school. These additional resources include:

- mortuary services (especially those with *trained* grief counseling and education personnel),
- veterans' centers (either federal centers or the local CBOs that exist in some parts of the country),
- mental health center personnel and/or in-patient psychiatric hospital crisis teams (who are *trained* in trauma and debriefing),
- individual therapists (who have specialized *training* and/or *experience* with trauma and debriefing).

Experience has shown that just because an individual claims to have expertise, that does not mean this is, in fact the case. Others may wish to be involved because of personal goals, such as publicity or the opportunity for research, which do not necessarily compliment the goals of the school. One need only ask school leaders who have experienced such a barrage of offers of "help." *Educators must verify all such claims.* In time of crisis, credibility and the trust of the community are essential.

Some locales may have none of the above services in close proximity, while others have many such services available. In either case, educators can help develop and coordinate the resources needed by the community to help the school with unexpected incidents that have often times overwhelmed existing support networks that were in place.

WHY "DEBRIEFING?"

At this point one might ask, "Why this emphasis on 'debriefing' when there are counselors in our schools and we have good counselors in our community?" It is my experience that the most constructive plan for all concerned is one which uses a common, consistent, flexible format to cope with a critical incident. School and community counselors are valuable assets but they may be entering an area counselors are valuable assets but they may be entering an area frought with hazards in dealing with a critical incident. Support must also be shown for the people providing the counseling and debriefing, whether they think they need it or not.

An example of this need may be seen in my own position with the Medical Response Team from Allen County based in Fort Wayne, Indiana. I am the CISD officer and the mortuary officer for that medical disaster team. Typically, there are two or three other CISD trained people who deploy with me and support my effort both in training situations and in actual deployment. These other CISD team members may be busy doing medical work, but they are there when I need them to support me. I have first hand experience of the truly critical importance of the emphasis on prevention and intervention because we were the first team Disaster Medical Assistance Team (DMAT) on site after Hurricane Andrew passed through the South Miami area. That episode provided a working example of what can be accomplished with prior planning and diligent work to construct a preventive base upon which to build. If this is not done, key people may be on different wavelengths or have different priorities during, or immediately after, a critical incident. If that should occur, the team will have to stop their efforts to sort out these differences in the midst of an already very stressful situation. This involves an unnecessary expenditure of time and effort by team members, and threatens the effectiveness of the team approach to the situation.

The majority of current CISD and Post-Traumatic Stress Disorder (PTSD) literature stress the prevention and intervention stages as the ideal place to invest your energy and time in order to help individuals to be resilient to PTSD. We cannot prevent PTSD, but we can help others, and ourselves, to be more resistent to it.

With the coordination of CISD type resources we can provide school staff, students, and their families with critical incident education. This can help them to be sensitized to their individual role in the process and familiarize them with the overall debriefing process so that it does not seem "foreign" to them when they might need assistance at a critical time. Planned CISD services represent community service at its best.

When an incident takes place combined support and cooperation are offered from all of these parties but circumstances may still make it difficult for some to cope. Because of a previous lack of planning, many of the working models around the country focus on postvention in the aftermath of an incident. That is, at best, a job half-done. Prevention and intervention are the areas that today offer the greatest opportunity. If a school community can do a better job of self-care and become, in a general way, inoculated as much as possible to the eventuality of a critical incident, then the work of the intervention and postvention stages will more likely create a healthy atmosphere in which people can heal. Even those individuals in the school community who have previously been traumatized can have an easier time recovering from an incident. A nurturing environment can enable them to respond to the challenge of this incident and to succeed in meeting it. All of the individuals in a coordinated response effort, no matter what their role, help to create a healing atmosphere rooted in cooperation. This is a sharp contrast to the squabbling over what to do, who will do it, how it will be done, how long it should take, where will it be done, etc. . . . etc. The cooperative/coordinated model of dealing with a school incident will maximize the potential for health and healing of the persons most affected by that incident. Intervention plans should be in place *before* an incident because as the magnitude of an incident grows, so does the difficulty index in regard to the healing process.

WHEN SHOULD THIS EFFORT BE MOBILIZED?

The decision to mobilize the efforts of the CISD team and other community resources depends on both the nature of the incident itself and the number of resources available. Schools have utilized CISD team resources in connection with the following incidents:

- suicides of members of the school community,
- homicides,
- hostage incidents,
- disasters—natural (flood, fire, earthquake) or man-made (explosion, violence, war),
- auto accidents/deaths,
- sports participation deaths.

Each of these incidents required a response. This was especially true when the incident took place in the school or on school grounds, but it would also apply should these events take place in a more peripheral fashion. The decision as to the appropriate level of response should be made by the school administration in cooperation with parents, when such lines of communication already exist. The CISD team coordinator, team members, school administration, parents and students (if appropriate) should play a role in guiding the duration, scope and limits of this activity and in determining whether available help should be requested from other regional resources.

GUIDELINES FOR RESPONSE PROTOCOLS

Protocols for the effective use of CISD type resources require flexibility, cooperation, and coordination of local and regional debriefing resources. It may also require additional expenditures to coordinate these different groups and individuals and to bring them all up to the appropriate level of knowledge and skill on such topics as CISD, trauma, death and dying, grief, etc.

One part of the protocol must address the *timely deployment* of these resources. After an incident, there is a window of opportunity that exists for approximately ninety-six hours in which debriefing can take place and be of maximum benefit. This time frame is critical. It is essential to have an agreed-upon method of activating and deploying the CISD team to avoid taking critical time to develop this component in the wake of an incident. This is frequently accomplished by utilizing the emergency service chain of command. A similar chain of command can be developed in our schools.

These guidelines are, of necessity, general in nature. The conditions and needs of an individual school or locale must be taken into account when developing specific protocols for response. One final word of caution; take the time and effort *now* to screen carefully the individuals who you will entrust with this process in your community. Be careful and knowledgeable consumers—even in your choice of volunteers.

There is an old military adage used here in slightly "modified" form: Proper Prior Planning Prevents Poor Performance. Many incidents that occur in the military are seen as critical. Even those events which are not critical are routinely used to train people to respond to those which are. Today's schools can be expected to encounter any of a number of possible crises. Are our children any less valuable than our soldiers? Do they not have as great a right to "proper prior planning?" More and more school communities are answering, yes!

CHAPTER 12

Helping Peers to Help Themselves: The Role of Peer Support in Times of Crisis[1]

Robert G. Stevenson

All members of a school community can need help and support in times of crisis. Typically, it is students who are the first ones targeted for assistance. However, a crisis plan will be incomplete if it sees students only as recipients of help. In many cases, these young people are the first ones to provide help and support to one another, and may even support staff and parents. When a student's mother died suddenly, the first one's there were two of her classmates. Her father said that the girl was better able to face what had happened from the time her friends arrived. After seeing his daughter's response, he asked the school to allow two of his son's friends to come to the home to be with him. Such help and support by students exists without formal training or organization. However, with training and support for their efforts, students can play an important role in the crisis plan of a school community.

When a personal or community crisis occurs, young people who know they need support may not seek it from traditional adult authority figures. Most often they turn first to their peers. Educators and counselors saw the ways in which students supported one another. These caring adults joined with student leaders to develop programs

[1]Some of the information contained in this chapter comes from the pamphlet "Adolescent Support In Schools: Touching All the Bases" (River Dell High School, 1987) by Robert G. Stevenson, Joseph Cafaro, and Claire Marino.

which offer formal training and support to these teen helpers. Through programs such as PLAN (Peer Leader Assistance Network), peer support has become a program to assist students who wish to be a source of help and understanding to each other in coping with many types of crises.

An example of such a peer support program exists at River Dell High School in Oradell, New Jersey. Approximately sixty eleventh and twelfth grade students (about 10% of the school's enrollment) are members of the school's Peer Listener Assistance Network. This network provides students in the high school with a safety net, where trained students reach out or respond to those in need with a caring attitude and appropriate referral skills. PLAN members have taken over a major part of the high school's suicide prevention program. They help with the orientation program for first year students and serve as "buddies" for students who transfer into the school during the academic year. PLAN also provides an outreach program which sends older teens to work with students in the middle school and in local elementary schools.

PLAN provides an atmosphere of understanding in which students can accept each other as they are, validate each other's experiences and feelings and offer support through troubled times. It also trains young people to assist in times of stress, both expected (new students arriving in the senior high school each year) and unexpected (the emotional aftermath of the sudden death of a student in gym class). Such preparation has created a group of students who can be a major help in times of crisis, if a role for these students has been made part of the school's crisis response plan *in advance.*

Through advance planning, PLAN students have taken on a central role in the Adolescent Suicide Awareness Program (ASAP) at River Dell. A central theme in this program is that each individual can be a powerful person in helping others by listening, by being aware of the warning signs of suicide and knowing when to refer a troubled peer to a professional. PLAN expands this concept. Through its members, PLAN helps to develop feelings of personal control and to increase positive feelings of self-worth among the students. In ASAP, the second part of the two-day program is run entirely by PLAN members. Their presence in the program has opened channels of communication among the students that would be difficult to duplicate with in a program run exclusively by adults. In a crisis which effects the whole school community, it can seem that there are never enough trained people to meet all of the needs that arise. Students can assume many roles in a crisis plan, freeing others to tackle those tasks which may be beyond the ability of teens to handle.

In many cases, the PLAN students at River Dell have referred a troubled youngster who then was seen and helped by a professional. On a daily basis PLAN provides peer support for students facing all the issues of growing up including the stress and loss a teenager may encounter. In a crisis, such referral skills can be invaluable.

There are those who are not comfortable with asking young people to offer support to peers at any time, and especially in times of crisis. In examining this concern, it is important to remember that these young people are *volunteers*, that they are *trained in appropriate responses*, *and* that they *have ongoing adult supervision and support*. One often-repeated objection can be met through a clear description of the role of these young people. In its early days, peer support was known as peer *counseling*. These young people may be peer listeners and may help peers to make contact with appropriate support professionals or organization, but they are *not* counselors. In any peer support program, this point must be made clear from the start to all parties. A young person who attempts to take on tasks better left to professionals may do more harm than good. Clarifying those responses which are or are not appropriate must be part of any peer support training.

GOALS

Peer support can be an important part of a school's crisis plan. The overall objective of such a crisis plan is to link together existing services (such as school counseling, community health services, police and fire services, religious leaders, and political leaders) and to draw on caring adults (such as teachers and parents) in order to help the members of the school community during and after a crisis. PLAN is on-going and, as such, not only complements existing services, but increases the school's opportunity to provide an atmosphere of concern for its students. It is the goal of the school to have someone there for any student who needs help. Since there are times when a student may be called on to fulfill that role, peer support programs seek to develop such students.

SELECTION PROCESS

The building of trust within a school community takes time. It is not a task that is easily done in the turmoil that often accompanies and follows a crisis. It is, therefore, desirable to have peer support programs in place in advance of any possible crisis and to include in that group representatives from many student groups as peer support members. A cross section of students breaks down stereotypes and enhances the potential success of reaching all members of the school community.

At River Dell, juniors and seniors interested in becoming PLAN members simply nominate themselves or classmates for the support program. Also, teachers and counselor are asked to point out natural leaders—students who seem to be respected by students (regardless of academic standing or extra-curricular participation). Students are also invited to join PLAN at an orientation meeting held at the beginning of the school year.

All interested students submit a personal statement about their strengths and possible weaknesses as a potential peer listener. Then, each student is interviewed by professional staff and previously installed PLAN members. During the interview, students are asked to describe how they would handle a possible support situation, such as a boy/girl conflict or a bereaved student. Their responses help the group to determine their abilities to be non-judgmental and resourceful, as well as trustworthy and confidential. Those students who wish to join but who, for some reason, may not be chosen for training in one-to-one support are still offered a role in PLAN in publicity (an ongoing program throughout the school year), or planning for programs by outside experts for PLAN members or the student body.

In addition to the screening process, all PLAN members who will offer one-to-one support must go through an initial training session.

TRAINING

The training program for PLAN members at River Dell was developed jointly by the school psychologist (Mr. Joseph Cafaro), a school counselor (Mrs. Claire Marino), and a classroom teacher (Dr. Robert Stevenson). The program involves a basic five-hour workshop to improve students' listening skills. Activities are designed to build a sharing environment and a sense of bonding among PLAN members. Specific listening skills that are stressed include:

- involvement,
- understanding,
- exploration,
- developing a plan of action.

During the initial training sessions, the students practice their listening skills by participating in role-plays that involve typical situations they may encounter. Some of the "roles" deal with peer pressure to use drugs, broken relationships, and parent discord. The PLAN members are critiqued on their use of the four stages of listening and are given suggestions by group members on how to improve. Another key element stressed to the students is that they are listeners, not therapists. Thus, specific information on when and where to refer troubled peers is included in the first training session.

An outline of a typical training session would typically include the following:

- *Overview of Program* (Goals, Activities, Timelines)—the trainers review the goals of peer support and seek to build a sense of group identity, provide information about listening skills and time to practice those skills, enable students to know when and where to refer a troubled peer, and reinforce the importance of confidentiality.
- *Group Activities* (to form group identity) include ice breakers, a non-verbal activity, a period of safe, brief self-disclosure, an experience of acceptance and mutual trust.
- *Effective Listening Skills*—This includes both large and small group experiences. There is a large group lecturette about involvement, exploration, understanding, and action. There is a role play of four stages by the trainers. In the small group experience some students role play and practice "listening skills" while others provide feedback on effectiveness.
- *Dinner Break: A Community Building Activity*—Students "prepare" and "serve" and share a meal, with the ingredients provided by the trainers.
- *Referral Skills*—Brainstorming of list of issues on problems that should be referred by peer support members to a professional. Specific names of individuals and groups, and the telephone numbers of school and community sources of help are given to each participant.
- *Group Activity*—This exercise offers closure to the training program. It also attempts to produce a product which can remind each participant of the training program and of their connection to each other and of the ideas and principals discussed during the program. Such an activity could include art work (developing a group logo or creating a poster to let the school know who these peer listeners are) or a poem, song, sculpture or other form of expression.
- *Wrap Up and Evaluation of Workshop*—Students grade the content and presentation of the evening's events. This training program has constantly been revised and improved through this input

by the participants themselves. The program ends after five hours. It is important to schedule closure so that the program does not run on in an opened manner, leaving participants with a impression of confusion or poor planning. This program is only a starting point for peer listeners. The end of this program is only the end of the beginning.

SCHEDULING

The evening scheduling of training has been a topic of much debate. It has been asked if training should be done during school hours, to show the emphasis placed on this work by the school, or on weekends, to show a commitment by the students. It was decided to keep the evening training sessions. The school does give time to the peer support program, but this school time is needed to meet with junior high school students and for other in-school programs. Students do give up weekend time for peer support, but weekends are already used to attend regional peer support training sessions. An evening meeting for the initial training session marks this program an special. It is the only part of the peer support program scheduled at this time. For these reasons, the evening schedule has been maintained.

Training of peer support students is continued during bi-monthly meetings. New skills are introduced and existing skills are reviewed and practiced by the students, In addition, professionals in other mental health areas are asked to speak to the peer support members on specific topics, such as AIDS, Planned Parenthood, Alcoholics Anonymous, or substance abuse.

Judging from comments made by PLAN members, they are highly satisfied with the training sessions. They feel that the emphasis on effective listening skills is most beneficial not only in one-to-one peer counseling, but in their everyday interaction with classmates at school.

When peer support was being considered for the school, a school-wide survey was conducted by a social studies instructor and a guidance counselor. In that poll, the students expressed a fear that violations of confidentiality would undermine the possible success of any such student group. The double-bind of confidentiality has been a major focus of the training program. Students are told that confidentiality is absolute *unless that student or someone else might be hurt by that silence.* In the years since the program of peer support began, there have been no violations of confidentiality or instances of inappropriate confidentiality (failing to make a needed referral to professionals). Such an incident could still occur, but the responsible and caring attitude of the peer listeners has been marked by caring and maturity and by behavior which has been both supportive and appropriate to their task.

SERVICES AND PROGRAMS

Members of peer support programs need to be aware of the full range of losses experienced by their peers. In addition to the death of parents, siblings and grandparents, they need to understand that there are other losses students frequently encounter. They include: divorce; not making a sports team; death of a pet; not being accepted to a college; a sibling going off to college; a friend moving away; and boyfriend/girlfriend breakup. There is also the possibility at any time that they may be called on to assist in a time of crisis.

It is not surprising that members of peer support programs are mostly frequently sought by peers facing the breakup of a romance. But whether for this loss or any other, these peer support members know that ways of helping include: listening and validating feelings, allowing the other to grieve and express hurt, and reaching out with support and concern while the other begins to rebuild. All of these skills can be used as part of a crisis plan. Recent storms in the South, floods in the Midwest and fires in the West have created crises that have had an impact on people of all ages. In many of these cases, the school has become a focal point for support during the crisis (where we have all seen photos or film of rows of cots in school gyms, cafeterias and classrooms) and afterward.

CONCLUSION

Peer support is based on a simple concept. Young people trust each other in their everyday sharing and "natural leaders" can fill the communication gap that may occur between adolescents and adults. Students who are "trained listeners" help weave a fabric of caring throughout a school. Everyday problems, as well as major crises, have the potential of being handled more effectively through this effort. If a program of peer support is established now to begin dealing with everyday problems, it will be there to be part of a crisis plan when a crisis occurs.

CHAPTER 13

Questions and Answers

The following questions and answers are representative of those most often asked by concerned adults about the ideas contained in the previous chapters.

GRIEF

What does a child "understand" about death and what role does age play?

ANSWER: Before age two, children have little or no understanding of death. If they are aware of anything, it is that someone they love and need is "missing." In the early school years, kindergarten to about third grade, they see death as "reversible." From about third grade to fifth or sixth grade, they "personify" death as a way of "avoiding" it. An adult understanding develops at about age ten.

What information about death is "essential" for a child to understand?

ANSWER: A young child should be helped to understand that the dead person no longer experiences anything (the body is *non-functional*), that the physical aspects of death last forever (death is *irreversible*), and that all living things will one day die (death is *universal*).

What should I tell our child / children about our thoughts and feelings surrounding the losses in our family? Is it alright for us to show our feelings about these losses even if we get upset in front of them?

ANSWER: It is very important to be honest with your child/children but do NOT give them any more information that they can handle (the Keep It Simple Principle!). Yes, it is alright for you to show your feelings in front of the child/children. In fact, it is part of being an effective role-model for them. Further more, it shows them that adults grieve too and that it is alright for adults to cry!

Why is it that people sometimes think or feel as if they are going crazy when they experience losses in their lives?

ANSWER: The grief process causes us to think or feel very out of control and render of unable to function the way we usually do. This can cause us to believe that we are going "crazy."

Why is it that I think or feel so "alone" in my grief?

ANSWER: When we are unable or unwilling to discuss our thoughts, feelings and behaviors with someone who will listen and validate them, we tend to withdraw and isolate ourselves from other people. This physical and emotional isolation can lead to a belief that we are alone in our loss.

Why do these things happen to me?...to anyone?

ANSWER: Why do bad things happen to good people? Well, life is not always fair or easy, but it *is* worth being alive! We can spend a lot of time trying to answer the "why" questions and get nothing but greater frustration. What we have to do is shift our focus to a different question...."What can I do to handle these situations in my life that are so painful?" Once we make this shift in focus our pain can become more manageable and we may feel less helpless. This is the first step toward the healing part of the grief process.

How can I avoid experiencing these grief reactions again?

ANSWER: You can't! The only way that you may not experience these reactions again, is if you never form attachments to any person, place or thing. Ask yourself if that is how you really want to live. Anytime that we decide to form attachments to a person, place or thing, we run the risk of having these grief reactions. Life is a risk and so are the relationships we choose to make in our lives.

Why does it hurt so much to love and to lose that love?

ANSWER: A book called *Lifetimes: A Beautiful Way To Explain Death To Children* repeats an important message throughout its text. This message is that "in life there are beginnings and endings and in between there is living." Even though love is a wonderful feeling it also has its painful side. Losing a person, place or thing we love can cause us incredible pain. In time, if we choose, we can learn from that pain and experience some new learning and personal growth.

Why do we need to wear a mask that helps us to pretend that we are doing alright?

ANSWER: Sometimes our losses become too much for us to handle and we need a way to step away from the pain of loss. Wearing a mask can help us to distance ourselves from this pain and may give us a time out from it all. To "look aside" briefly in this way is alright and should not be viewed as being in denial. Detaching ourselves gives us a chance to re-charge our batteries and to experience some relief from the pain. We need these masks. They are useful tools to help us through this difficult process.

SUICIDE

What can I do if I think or feel so overwhelmed by grief that I start to think about suicide?

ANSWER: First, it is essential that you realize that suicidal thoughts are common enough to be considered "normal," but suicidal actions are NOT. However, it is NOT alright to continue with these thoughts so that a pattern develops. In order to help yourself through this difficult time, you MUST risk reaching out to someone that you trust and who will listen and validate your reactions. You may first only be able to talk to a friend. A friend can help by listening and then by getting the person to get professional help. Reaching out for help is a sign of personal *courage*, not weakness. Please remember the oft quoted observation that suicide is a permanent solution to a temporary problem!

What can I do or say to help a friend who is talking or acting as if he/she is contemplating suicide?

ANSWER: First, it is important to remember that you are *not* responsible for another person's life. But you can still be a special friend by getting them some professional help. Even if they may have asked you NOT to tell anyone, do not keep that confidence. This is too much for you to handle on your own. If they get angry at you for doing this, it is better to have them angry at you than to have them dead. If they are angry they may some day forgive you, if they are dead they never will. Remember to validate their feelings . . . don't tell them to "stop being silly" and don't ever ignore this behavior or treat it as if they are just seeking attention. Ask "Is this the worst things have ever been for you?" If they say no, you can remind them they have had the ability to cope with worse situations in the past. If they say yes, you know that this person is at risk.

What should I avoid saying or doing if I think that someone I am with may be considering suicide?

ANSWER: Do not "challenge" the person by saying that s/he is not serious. Do not weigh the "pros" and "cons" of suicide. This could be a signal that there are times when suicide is acceptable and could actually give a person just the "permission" they need to act on their thoughts/feelings.

What two key issues do educators, parents and students themselves need to know to assist a suicidal teenager?

ANSWER: Educators, parents and students need to be able to:

- *identify* students at risk for suicidal behavior, and
- *refer* the troubled adolescent for adult professional assistance.

Does talking about suicide in school cause students to make an attempt?

ANSWER: Research and clinical experience demonstrate that addressing the tragic reality of adolescent suicide with adolescents *does not* precipitate attempts. Talking about the issue encourages them to understand and handle suicidal crises appropriately.

What are the three goals of comprehensive school based suicide prevention programs?

ANSWER: The three goals of school based suicide prevention programs are:

- Prevention education for the entire school community
- Intervention procedures and programs for managing suicidal ideation, threats and attempts.

- Postvention strategies to: 1) assist the school reentry of student who has attempted suicide, and 2) manage the aftermath of a completed suicide.

What are some of the reasons a school might resist instituting a suicide prevention program?

ANSWER: Schools may resist implementing suicide prevention programming for a combination of realistic concerns such as an overcrowded calendar, teacher resistance, lack of sufficient funding, appropriate materials, or due to misunderstandings such as the fear that talking about suicide will precipitate an attempt or that their school or community is invulnerable to suicide.

SCHOOLS AND HIV/AIDS

How can the claim be made that a HIV infected person or a person with AIDS is not a threat to the school population?

ANSWER: It is based on the nine separate studies, according to the Centers for Disease Control, which indicated that no family member of the over 70,000 AIDS patients identified to date has been reported to have contracted AIDS by casual contact (sharing a household).

What is the best resource for information on HIV/AIDS?

ANSWER: The Centers for Disease Control (CDC) have been tracking HIV/AIDS since it began in the United States. They are regarded as the most reliable source of accurate and up-to-date information.

What evidence exists to support the claim that teenagers in the U.S. are a high risk group for HIV infection?

ANSWER: Over 60 percent of high school seniors are sexually active: 40 percent of females become pregnant before age twenty; STD rates for teens are of epidemic proportions. Also, research shows that over one-third of high school students come from homes where abuse, violence, and drugs/alcohol are a problem. This group is at even higher risk for acting out sexually as well as multiple related problems.

Why do we have to teach HIV education in our schools?

ANSWER: Federal and state laws and guidelines require HIV prevention and risk reduction education.

SCHOOLS AND THE MILITARY

My child is worried that his father will die while he is gone? Is it okay to tell him that his father will be back?

ANSWER: No, you should not tell him that his father will not die because you cannot guarantee this. In the event that his father was killed, your child might feel that you had lied to him, and that he could no longer trust you. Tell him that you hope his father will return. If you have a religious background, you can encourage the child to pray with you each day for his father. Explain to him also, that you are there to take care of him, and other people in the family (grandparents, aunts, uncles) also care about him, and would take care of him. He needs to be assured of his care and safety during this time.

My child appears captivated by the news coverage about the war. Should I allow him to watch this?

ANSWER: The answer for this depends on the age and maturity of the child. Some news coverage is acceptable for an older child to watch. Even younger children can watch the news if you are there to explain what is going on and to calm fears they may have about their parent's safety. However, extensive news watching is not good for any child. It may cause fears to arise that were not already present. Children may also become so involved in watching the news that they forget to be children—to go outside, to play with their friends. These activities are critical, especially during the stressful time when a parent is on a war-related assignment. Watch some war coverage with your child, answer questions, then turn it off.

My child asks a lot of questions about the war. She hears about it at school and her father is getting ready to leave. I am afraid to answer her questions, because I think it will just make her more worried. What should I do?

ANSWER: It is important to answer a child's questions. Answer them with honesty and with consideration for her age and maturity. Simple answers to her questions can relieve fears that may be building up. Remember to just answer the question. Do not give extensive information that may not be related to what she is asking. When you avoid answering questions, your daughter will only make up answers for her questions, and her answers may be much worse than reality.

SCHOOLS, SUPPORT GROUPS AND BEREAVED ADOLESCENTS

What are some of the factors that can hinder an adolescent's grief process?

ANSWER: The grief process can be hindered when others, such as parents, teachers and/or peers:

- do not listen to what these adolescents are saying,
- do not validate their thoughts and feelings,
- deny the individuality of the grief process,
- suggest that there is only one way to grieve,
- suggest that there is a set time for the grief process.
- do not recognize that this adolescent may be facing multiple losses.

How does the peer support group facilitate the grief process for adolescents?

ANSWER: A peer support groups provides an opportunity for adolescents to meet one another, to share their thoughts and feelings, to understand that the grief process is "normal" but not comfortable, and to learn (or re-learn) coping skills and new behaviors that will facilitate the grief process.

Why is it acceptable to put adolescents of different ages in the same peer support group?

ANSWER: The different ages of adolescents in these groups illustrates that loss has no age restrictions and can affect all of us no matter what our age. Older adolescents often become like big brothers and sisters to the younger adolescents in the group. That kind of connection offers the opportunity for the older adolescents to fulfill a supportive, nurturing role and to feel sense of worth. The younger adolescents experience a sense of belonging rather that feeling isolated and misunderstood.

Why is it alright to put adolescents with different losses in the same peer support group?

ANSWER: Putting adolescents with different losses together in the same group introduces the concept that there are numerous kinds of losses with which adolescents must learn to cope. It also suggests that we do not have to compete with one another as to whose loss is worse. This introduces the idea that the grief "process" is primarily the same no matter what the loss. However, some types of death, such as death by suicide or murder, are often a "double whammy" for the adolescents who have experienced this kind of loss.

How do you get adolescents to attend the peer support group on a regular basis (every session)?

ANSWER: The participants are told that this is NOT a drop-in group and that they need to be there every session because it is not fair to ask others to share their thoughts and feelings in the group and then to have to repeat these thoughts and feelings in another session if someone in the group was away at the last session.

Why won't our child/children talk to us about the losses in their lives?

ANSWER: Adolescents begin to stop telling their parents their innermost thoughts and feelings because they are trying to make the developmental adjustments that are referred to as "separation-individuation process."

Why are the adolescents in these groups told to NOT discuss any information that is shared in the group with anyone, including parents, outside of the group?

ANSWER: Adolescents in these groups are told to NOT discuss any information that is shared in the group because confidentiality and having a safe place to risk sharing this information is essential to the group process and group dynamics.

Why is it so hard to be different than other kids when you are an adolescent?

ANSWER: Sometimes we call this "peer pressure". This is a time in life when you are trying to figure out who you are and what you want to do with your life? It can be a very confusing time and often being "different" is looked down upon by adolescents. It may take a lot of guts to be different and to stand up for what you believe. As the drug awareness programs say, "Just Say No!"

Why is that I often think or feel or act as if I am never ever going to be happy again? . . . that these grief reactions are never ever going to change?

ANSWER: The emotions that accompany loss hurt, and the healing of the grief process takes time.

- HOPE
- HAVE PATIENCE
- SHARE YOUR THOUGHTS, FEELINGS, AND ACTIONS WITH OTHERS
- RISK CARING/LOVING/ATTACHING AGAIN
- BELIEVE IN YOURSELF
- LEARN ABOUT THE GRIEF PROCESS

All of the above are tools that can help you to be happy again and to change. During the initial phases of the grief process your reactions (reactive phases) are expressed through *protest, despair* and *detaching*. Once you try to understand your losses, you begin to move toward the next phase that is referred to as meaning. During this phase we are trying to make some sense out of the losses that we have experienced and to begin shifting from asking WHY to the WHAT NOW phase which will enable us to *explore, hope* and *invest* in ourselves and in new relationships. These phases help us to be more proactive and to begin the healing process. It is at this time that we begin to be happy and to change.

SPECIAL CRISIS SECTION

Guidelines for Dealing with Crisis

This section is intended to offer a quick overview of information contained in the preceding chapters. It is intended to offer direction when faced with an immediate crisis or emergency, when time may not be available to review the longer presentation. As a general rule, parents and educators can encourage schools to take the following steps to prepare for a crisis:

Create a School/District Steering Committee to develop, write, distribute, and review a Crisis Management Plan.

Create a task force of educators, parents, and community members to be the focal point of intervention efforts when crises do occur. Each person should know the role he/she will play in a given crisis situation. This group is sometimes called a Crisis Response Team.

Develop protocols for use when crises occur. These protocols identify in advance key individuals, resources, and support groups. Procedural guidelines should make clear the circumstances that lead to activation, by whom, duration of operation and any specified limitation.

Develop and implement in service educational programs for teachers, students, and parents dealing with those crises which currently exist or for which the school community is at risk.

Identify all local and regional resources for support: Contact should be established with community mental health agencies, Critical Incident Stress Debriefing teams, or community Crisis Response Teams.

Develop and maintain *an ongoing program of staff development,* with parent and community outreach components, to prepare all members of the school community to be resources in crises.

Open and maintain lines of communication among all parties, teachers, counselors, parents, and students which can be used to convey good news as well as bad and can combat the potential harm caused by rumor or ignorance of important information.

Debrief the debriefers: Support those who offer support so that they can continue to be a resource for both school and community.

GUIDELINES FOR SCHOOL BASED CRISIS MANAGEMENT

Definitions

Crisis: a serious or decisive state of things. In terms of an individual or group, crisis in an acute, emotional upset arising from situational, developmental, or social sources and resulting in a temporary inability to cope through usual problem solving devices.

Emergency: an unforeseen combination of circumstances that call for immediate action, often with life and death implications.

Stress: the tension or pressure that is felt when one is in crisis.

Crisis management: a process in which all the aspects of working through a crisis are utilized to the point of crisis elimination, resolution or prevention.

Crisis counseling: an aspect of the crisis management process focusing particularly on the emotional ramifications of the crisis. The person who engages in crisis counseling must be one who has formal preparation in counseling techniques.

Crisis intervention: that aspect of the management process that focuses on the resolution of the immediate problem through the use of personal, social, environmental, and sometimes material resources.

Crisis prevention: the process of reducing the onset of acute, emotional upset experienced in a crisis by developing educational programs that enable a person to examine her/his coping behaviors, resources and skill of assessment.

Crisis postvention: a process of damage assessment and damage control. It is a process of assisting the person to learn how to live with the aftermath and all its effects.

Grief crisis intervention: a process that employs grief counseling techniques with selected crisis intervention procedures.

PLANNING CRISIS MANAGEMENT PROTOCOLS

These protocols should include:

- identification of the individual(s) who is response for the provision of service;

- description of the recommended qualifications a crisis intervener, including a description of the type of academic work and clinical experience desired of someone assuming this role;
- types of crises which would necessitate the activation of the plan and personnel;
- a plan of evaluation for follow-up of initial support, and effectiveness of the intervention; and
- the identification of the school or district person to whom all support personnel are accountable.

PREPARATION OF STAFF

Training should include:
- an examination of one's own death related concerns and issues;
- understanding the grief process and the long term manifestations of unresolved grief;
- understanding of disenfranchised, complicated and pathological grief.

Attitudes that should be present in a crisis worker include:
- an acceptance of a non-judgmental response to persons different from self and toward controversial issues—not discussing the moral rightness or wrongness of abortion with a person,
- a balanced, realistic attitude toward oneself in the helper role—not expecting to rescue or save everyone whom one assists,
- a realistic and humane approach to death, dying and self-destructive behavior;
- being able to deal with emotional issues like AIDS, and
- a coming to terms with one's own feelings about death, dying and loss.

Skills it would be advantageous if the crisis support person:
- is able to apply the techniques of formal crisis management including the skills of assessment, planning, implementation, and evaluation;
- possesses good communication skills including the ability to listen actively, question discretely, respond empathetically, and advise and direct appropriately;
- is able to mobilize community resources effectively and efficiently; and
- is able to keep accurate records.

Competencies of Crisis Interveners: The essential competencies for grief crisis interveners include:

- Knowledge of self
- Knowledge of the subject matter
- Knowledge of communication skills
- Knowledge of the student
- Knowledge of the total environment
- Knowledge of the principles of curriculum design
- Knowledge of what is possible in the classroom

SUMMARY

In summary, a list of suggested guidelines for a school based grief crisis management program should include:

- confront do not attempt to deny or avoid the crisis, the problem will not disappear on its own;
- prepare in anticipation do not prepare in crisis;
- develop inclusive support programs do not create policies of exclusion;
- seek qualified personnel do not appoint untrained people;
- modify protocol based on assessment and evaluation of process and not on the unsubstantiated perceptions of a few; and
- include care for the crisis team members as part of the planned support program do not assume that the caregiver needs no care.

GUIDELINES FOR INFORMING AN INDIVIDUAL STUDENT OF A LOSS

Who Should Inform the Student?

- The student should be told by someone he/she sees as an authority figure.
- Someone who has a close relationship with the student (teacher, nurse, counselor, or fellow student) should be with the student and should be able to remain after the student receives the news.

Where Should the Student be Told?

- The student should be taken to a place where he/she can have *privacy*.
- The student should be able to sit or to lie down if necessary.

How should the student be told?

- The student should be told what has happened in a quiet, simple, and direct manner.
- Platitudes or religious symbolism should be avoided.
- The child's questions should be answered openly and honestly but unnecessary details need not be volunteered.
- Emotions and feelings should not be avoided.
- The wishes of the family, if they are known, should be respected as much as possible.

How Will a Student react?

- After a student has received the news, he or she may have any of a number of possible reactions. Educators must remember that there is no one "correct" response.
- The student should not be left alone.
- If the student remains silent, inform him/her that it is all right to speak about feelings.
- It is essential that staff reaction to a student not appear judgmental.

Who Else Should be Informed?

- The family should be aware of what the student was told and all of the child's teachers, the school nurse, and school counselors should be informed of the situation as soon as possible.

GUIDELINES FOR INFORMING GROUPS OF STUDENTS

Where Should the Students be Told?

- Large group presentations are almost always less beneficial for individual students. Whenever possible, students should receive the news of a crisis situation in familiar surroundings with people they know and trust. The classroom offers such a setting.

How Should the Students be Told?

- Preselected staff members will be sent to inform all students of the event(s) that has occurred.
- Not every educator will be comfortable performing such a task and this must be determined in advance.

- A team of educators (called a "crisis response team" in some districts) should receive additional training concerning student needs in times of grief and/or stress.
- The same information should be given to all students.
- The information should be given in a calm, direct manner and the team members should stay to assist the classroom teacher in answering questions and addressing feelings and reactions.
- The nurse should not be sent to inform students since some students may experience physical distress or have specific somatic complaints and will need the nurse to be available to perform her primary task as a medical professional.

How Will the Students React?

- While it is difficult to predict the reaction of an individual student, the reaction of *groups* of students is predictable.
- Students will feel sad or angry and will express these feelings.
- Students may feel guilty and seek to withdraw from interaction with peers or teachers.
- Students may not appear to feel anything at all. Some students may actually not be affected by the news or feel any personal involvement. However, there are students who *appear* uninvolved but are actually seeking to mask thoughts or feelings with which they are uncomfortable.
- It is essential that students be helped to understand that virtually all of these reactions are "normal" because, however the individual student reacts, it is a response others share.
- The intensity of individual reactions may be a cause for concern. A school protocol must provide assistance for those students who need individual support.
- Training and workshops should be provided for counselors, social workers, school nurses and interested teachers on a regular basis.

Who Else Should be Informed?

- All staff members must be kept informed of the details of events related to this crisis.
- Parents must be kept informed of the actions taken in school and of the events which affect their children.
- Community leaders (religious leaders, health professionals, uniformed services, and political leaders) should also be part of the information network.

- All communication must be two-way. School officials and teachers must solicit and be responsive to input from parents and the community as a whole.

What Issues can Complicate Student Reaction and/or School Response?

- Certain events have been found to be factors which may produce complicated student reactions in times of crisis. The type of death can produce a grief reaction which is different from that which follows a death caused by illness or accident.

GUIDELINES FOR ASSISTING STUDENTS IN CRISIS

Listen: Listen to what these young people are actually saying. Do not be distracted by thinking of possible future answers or actions while they are still telling their stories.

Allow Time For Staff Members To Meet With Students: Time must be set aside so that students can receive support when they need it and not according to some impersonal schedule.

Identify and List Issues which the Student Wishes to Address: This would include both the present crisis and past issues with which the student is still dealing. The length of such a list does not matter. A long list may appear frightening, but it can show a young person his/her strength is coping with all of these issues.

Establish Priorities: Ask, "What do *you* want to deal with first?" This is a starting point in having the young person identify the meaning that he/she has attributed to each event.

Seek to Understand How the Young Person Views this Crisis: Has it created a VOID? Is it an ENEMY? Is it a GAIN? Is this crisis ACTUAL (in the past or present) or ANTICIPATED (a possible future event)?

Help the Young Person Focus on One Issue at a Time: Avoid the overwhelming situation of trying to deal with all things at once or the confusion of moving too quickly from one issue to another.

Remind the Young Person that Each of Us has Both a Right and a Responsibility to Let Others Know of Our Losses if We Expect Them to Act toward Us in an "Appropriate" Way in Times of Crisis: If a loss has made a person different in some way and others are unaware of the loss, it may not be possible for them to act toward that person in an appropriate way. If the person needs support, he/she has a responsibility to let others know of the loss.

If that person needs to speak of the loss, he/she has a right to do so.

Remember that the School's Function is to Educate the "Whole Person: These young people bring past histories and personal issues which have a major effect on the learning process. Despite the many changes taking place in today's world, parents are still the first teachers of their children and are a key factor in determining the stability, values and mores in a child's life. However, there are many areas in which educators and parents can work together for the benefit of the children about whom they both care.

GUIDELINES FOR PREPARING A SCHOOL FOR CRISIS MANAGEMENT: THE STEERING COMMITTEE

The keys to successful crisis management are *pre-planning* and *preparation.* The primary responsibility for these falls to a steering committee. Once a steering committee has been formed, its tasks include:

- *Defining* what is considered to be a crisis,
- Determining appropriate *Levels of Response,*
- Establishing *Goals* for crisis management,
- Evaluating *Levels of Resistance,*
- Determine the impact of *Community Profile Characteristics,*
    - these characteristics typically include: geography, cultural and ethnic diversity, political and social climate, religious and philosophical implications, language, socio-economic status, available community resources, and other unique community characteristics.
- Collect *existing crisis plans* from the district or schools and review these existing plans.
- Determine *Chain of Command*
- Select *Crisis Response Team* members and assign their roles.
- Assign roles to *Staff Members*
- Plan for *Notification* of the members of the school community
    - this plan should include a telephone tree; procedures for notification of staff and an emergency staff meeting; plans for notification of students, families, and community officials; and a plan for dealing with media.
- Make provisions for *additional help* from outside resources or additional staff

- Write, distribute and support a *Crisis Management Plan*
- Plan to conduct a Post-crisis Evaluation.

GUIDELINES WHEN SUICIDE EFFECTS THE SCHOOL COMMUNITY

The basic goal of Crisis Intervention is to *reduce anxiety* and promote *effective problem solving* and prevent ineffective or destructive responses to crises. This is accomplished by providing timely and efficient *support* and *structure* to affected individuals and systems. It cannot be overemphasized that this must be done through planning *prior to the occurrence of any crisis.* The following steps should be included in any school plan:

1. School administrations must be familiar with and able to call upon community resources, including police, medical, mental health, and other relevant emergency personnel.
2. Referral and shared response arrangements should be explicitly developed among the school and community officials. This would be part of the Crisis Management Plan.
3. All school personnel should be thoroughly familiar with school resources (exactly who to contact in the case of possibly at-risk students, attempts or completions) and how these should be accessed.
4. If any adult in the school becomes aware of the *possibility that a student is suicidal,* s/he will contact the designated school official(s) who will initially talk with (assess) the student. The designated school official may then refer the student for further assessment or treatment. Parents are *always* contacted concerning the referral.
5. Students who are concerned about the possible suicidality of a peer should be told to contact *any* adult in the school community, all of whom should know the appropriate steps to take.
6. In the event of a suicide attempt by a student in the school, specific steps should be taken to obtain immediate professional (medical and/or mental health) assistance, notify the parents, and provide appropriate assistance to other students who are aware of the attempt. Support for other students could range from support for one or a few peers to postvention procedures for the entire school.
7. If a school official becomes aware of a student's suicide attempt off school grounds they should establish contact with the medical/ mental health providers and again provide appropriate assistance to those who are aware of the attempt.

8. In the event of a suicide completion, standard postvention procedures should be initiated *immediately.* It cannot be assumed that only *some* students need to be helped. This is often an understandable attempt on the part of well-intentioned adults to attempt to limit the scope of the problem, but in the aftermath of a completed suicide *all* students, as survivors of suicide, are at greater risk.

GUIDELINES FOR HELPING SURVIVORS OF SUICIDE

In the wake of a completed suicide, educators should be prepared to:

- *Talk about it:* Allowing students to talk about a problem is not likely to make a problem worse and it might make things better.
- *Explain the facts as you know them, and answer rumors:* Since many people seek information in the wake of a loss as a way of feeling *in control,* stories can spread rapidly . . . and many of these stories may be untrue. Stopping rumors helps to avoid unnecessary additional pain. Providing factual information establishes a relationship of trust which may be needed in the future.
- *Promote positive attitudes and positive solutions:* Suicide has been called a permanent "solution" to what may be a temporary problem. Stress positive ways of solving problems or of enduring the pain that follows a loss. Do not try to deal with student problems or concerns immediately, unless a student wishes to do so.
- *Acknowledge the change(s) this death has caused, but do not* validate the suicide: Change is a word that describes reality and avoids negative implications. Focusing on change allows non-judgmental discussion to occur. Discuss how things have changed for the survivor(s). Remember that each person is a unique individual with a personal perspective on what has happened and how it will effect him/her. Do not attempt to present the deceased as being "better off" and do not weigh the pros and cons of suicide.
- *Do* not *romanticize, but* do commemorate the death: Suicide clusters are a concern, but the messages sent by doing nothing may be far worse than the impact of anything we do or say.
- *Help survivors to remember the* complete *individual:* No one is all good or all bad. After a suicide there is a tendency among some survivors to portray the deceased as one-dimensional. It is beneficial to remember people as they were, not as we wish they had been.
- *Record dates of deaths so that there can be special vigilance on anniversaries:* Survivors face special stress and may be at greater risk of self-injury on the anniversary of a loss. Staff members should

be aware of the extra pressures which can affect the individual at such a time.

- *Take time to help the helpers:* The time to plan for an event of this type is *before* it occurs. *Staff members are also survivors.* There must also be a way for staff members to express and to process their own feelings and reactions.

GUIDELINES WHEN VIOLENCE EFFECTS THE SCHOOL COMMUNITY

1. A "Crisis Team" is assembled to put into place a response. Ideally, this has already been done and the team's plan will only have to be initiated.
2. Teachers are assembled to be given concise information on the event, allowed to voice concerns (as time allows) and to have their questions answered about the event. They then establish the details of the school response. They can draw on any school procedures already in place for crises.
3. Teachers will relate details of the event to students in small groups or classes. Small meetings will take place between members of the Crisis Team and students to allow students to get over their "shock" and to speak about (externalize) their thoughts and feelings. Students with special problems and concerns should be identified for immediate help and/or follow-up.
4. Plans for rumor control should be initiated with a contact person available to students, staff, and members of the community outside of the school.
5. Students and staff will decide on appropriate follow-up for the school community . . . stressing non-violent responses and problem solving.
6. After some time has passed, there should be specific follow-up by crisis team members with students to allow further venting of strong emotions, if needed, and to reinforce non-violent methods of problem solving.

GUIDELINES FOR COPING WITH MILITARY CRISES

I. Pre-Separation:

   1. When a war breaks out, and there is a family member leaving on a military-related assignment, tell children in terms they will understand. Do not exaggerate or give them more information than they can handle.

2. Explain why the parent is leaving, why his/her job is important.
3. Let children be involved, if they want to, in helping a parent prepare to leave.
4. Do not watch extensive TV coverage with children present.

II. During Separation:
1. Physical and emotional reactions can be expected during a war-caused separation.
2. Support from friends, military, and schools can be very helpful during this time.
3. Do not concentrate on the war. Continue to do family oriented activities. Children have a greater need to know they are cared for during this time.

III. Post-Separation:
1. Remember that it will take children and adults time to adjust to a parent's return.
2. Children may be hesitant to go to a returning parent, and patience will be needed to blend as a family unit.

CRISIS PLAN FOR THE RELIGIOUS SCHOOL COMMUNITY

Note: For the purposes of this section, we will use the example of a death as a crisis in the Religious School community.

1. A "Crisis Team" is assembled to put into place a response.
2. Teachers are assembled to be given concise information on the death, and counseled to deal with their emotions and traumas. They then work out the details of how the school will respond. Step 2 is most effective if it is completed *before* a crisis occurs.
3. Small meetings will take place with members of the Crisis Team and students to allow students to get over the "shock" and to emote.
4. Religious mourning customs will be observed, followed by a discussion of their value. Students will share ideas for possible new "customs" and liturgy which might be created to answer specific needs.
5. On significant occasions (e.g., one month or one year later), or at some special event when the absence of the deceased will be felt, there will be a need to revisit the emotions some people are experiencing.

GUIDELINES FOR DEVELOPING AN HIV/AIDS POLICY

It is not the purpose of a school HIV/AIDS Policy to provide detailed medical information. That information is constantly changing and is best explained by health care professionals. The HIV/AIDS policy adopted by a local school board for its district will be expected to:

- facilitate communication among key individuals and groups around issues related to HIV infection,
- articulate the societal values of the school district and community,
- establish a plan of action in policy and procedures for dealing with a student or staff member with HIV infection and other issues which may arise.
- clearly state how federal and state laws are to be implemented in the district,
- establish a base of support to be used if questions and/or criticism arise, and
- provide a meaningful opportunity for community and school to work together to foster positive behavior which is aimed at preventing the spread of HIV.

GUIDELINES FOR IMPLEMENTING AN HIV/AIDS POLICYMAKING PROCESS

Step 1. Gather existing information on policies, laws, and medical information.

Step 2. Identify all possible sources of assistance from the local to the national level.

Step 3. Form the steering committee that will develop the policy including: a broad range of community representatives to get diverse opinions and support, medical and legal experts, school representatives including union and/or association representatives.

Step 4. Educate the committee and the school board about HIV infection and other pertinent issues.

Step 5. Identify policy issues that must be addressed. First find out which issues are already covered by federal and state laws, then develop a list of additional topics that must be addressed.

Step 6. Prepare a first draft of the policy. Have committee members share this draft with their constituencies, gather opinions, and report back to the full committee.

Step 7. Prepare the final draft of the policy.

Step 8. Present the draft to the school board. Begin the policy adoption process, which may include public hearings.
Step 9. Inform the community about the policy.
Step 10. Set guidelines for periodically reviewing and evaluating the policy.

ACTION PLAN TO PREVENT OR MANAGE AN IMMEDIATE HIV/AIDS CRISIS

1. If a staff member becomes aware of the AIDS infected student, s/he should immediately contact the building principal or superintendent. All parties should be aware of pertinent regulations concerning student privacy and documentation should be kept to document that student/staff rights were protected.
2. A designated school official should confer with a parent/guardian or, if appropriate, the student.
3. If permission is received from the parent/guardian (in writing), the designated school official should confer with the primary health care provider.
4. If no questionable behavior or medical conditions exist, appropriate team members should be notified. The identity of the student should be disclosed only if legally appropriate.
5. As needed (and if legally appropriate) meet with above staff members and family/student to:
   a. discuss the continuance of educational programs and the need to build a support system for the student,
   b. discuss the need for staff in-service education,
   c. discuss the need for student education,
   d. discuss the need to plan a response to possible media intrusion,
   e. to initiate a district plan for rumor control.
6. Determine the HIV infected person has a communicable disease and plan for appropriate schooling to support the student.

ADDITIONAL CONSIDERATIONS RELATED TO HIV/AIDS ISSUES

In addition to the steps mentioned in the previous action plan, the following suggestions may be pertinent:

- Act with confidence to prevent a vacuum becoming filled with destructive leadership.

- Network with other community leaders, agencies such as law enforcement, hospitals, mental health agencies, social services, and crisis telephone lines.
- Make certain that confidentiality procedures are failsafe.
- "Be prepared to deliver intensive in-service and community education programs to the school/community in crisis." Take nothing for granted; use knowledgeable medical authorities, and expect to explain even "basic" information and answer questions about HIV infection and AIDS.
- "Recognize the potential minority dimensions of the issue. . . . It is important to stress that HIV is transmitted by risky *behavior,* not by 'risk groups.' Anyone can be infected if they engage in activities that may expose them to HIV."
- "Identify an expert in conflict resolution in case one is needed. . . . Superintendents and administrators who have already resolved AIDS-related conflicts in their communities can be particularly helpful."

GUIDELINES FOR A MEDIA LIAISON/SPOKESPERSON

1. See that *consistent* messages are given out.
2. Reassure the community through the media that the situation is being handled appropriately and competently.
3. Continue to build rapport with the media and to reinforce the importance of privacy/confidentiality for all parties.
4. Initiate *rumor control.* Check that all statements to the media contain accurate information. [In HIV/AIDS situations be sure that press releases contain medically and legally correct information.]
5. Prepare press releases which state the district policies, procedures, and responses. This can be done in a general way in advance of a crisis and the details can be filled in as needed.
6. Answer all questions related to student safety so that community members will understand that the school is acting in this crisis to protect all students and staff. [In issues related to HIV/AIDS, explain and reinforce the concept of *casual contact* and the research which supports the stand that such contact poses no threat to the others in the school or community.]
7. Indicate that *harassment or exploitation by the media will NOT be tolerated* in any form.
8. Set limits concerning presence of media on campus. Designate set times and places for media contacts. Be sure all media contacts are first directed to the designated spokesperson.

ISSUES RELATED TO LIFE THREATENING ILLNESS

I. *Individual Issues:* an individual/family facing life-threatening illness, including HIV/AIDS, typically chooses one of three possible options. They can:
   - Remain totally private,
   - Share confidential information on a limited basis,
   - Make their condition public.

   These young people may need support groups, and referrals to organizations that can assist them in coping with their diagnosis, prognosis, and specific challenges.

II. *Student Issues* related to life-threatening illness of a classmate include: dealing with feelings, physical problems, confidentiality, and issues involving family, friends, and caregivers.

III. *School Issues* may include:
   - confidentiality,
   - privacy,
   - consequences of a specific condition for the learning process,
   - prolonged student absence and re-entry, and
   - staff involvement and responses.

   There are some similarities, as well as distinct differences, when these issues are compared with those related to HIV/AIDS. One policy will not be able to be used with all types of chronic or life-threatening illness, and a district would be wise to have at least two types of planned responses.

Contributors

ROBERT STEVENSON has taught a death education course to the students of River Dell High School in Oradell, New Jersey for over twenty years and is co-chairman of the Seminar on Death at Columbia University. He is a nationally certified death educator and grief counselor who has been widely published on topics related to loss and grief. He is active in both the International Work Group On Death, Dying and Bereavement (I.W.G.) and the Association for Death Education and Counseling (A.D.E.C.). He is a graduate of the College of the Holy Cross (B.A.) and holds master's degrees from Fairleigh Dickinson University (M.A.T.) and Montclair State College (M.A.) and a doctoral degree (Ed.D.) from Fairleigh Dickinson.

Dr. Stevenson has written curricula for health and death education courses and has been honored for his work as an educator and counselor by: The New Jersey Professional Counselors' Association, the New Jersey Governor's Office, United States Chess Federation, National Council for the Social Studies, and is listed in Who's Who Among America's Teachers and Who's Who Among Human Service Professionals. He was honored in 1993 by A.D.E.C. with their Death Educator Award for significant contributions to the field.

SANDRA ELDER is a certified psychologist in private practice in British Columbia, Canada. She holds a Master's Degree (M.Ed.) from the University of Alberta and is currently a doctoral candidate in Counseling Psychology at the University of Victoria. She is a founder of the Living Through Loss Program to assist bereaved teens in the Greater Victoria schools.

DR. JOHN KALAFAT is currently a Professor of Psychology at Spaulding University, Louisville, Kentucky. Professor Kalafat's experience includes faculty position at Florida State, Fairleigh Dickinson and Rutgers Universities. He was the cofounder and director of a regional crisis center, director of a university counselling center, Director of Consultation and Education for a CMHC and Director of Training for

St. Clare's Medical Center in Denville, New Jersey. John has authored numerous journal articles regarding youth at risk and is coauthor of *Lifelines,* a school based suicide prevention curriculum. Dr. Kalafat currently serves as Cochair of the School Program Committee of the American Association of Suicidology.

WILLIAM LEE, JR. was born in Charleston, South Carolina and spent his youth in Boston, Massachusetts. He is a graduate of Harvard University and a member of the Harvard Chapter of Phi Beta Kappa. Founder and senior consultant/trainer of Implosion, Inc., he is an international presenter of programs related to death, loss and violence. He hold licenses as a Family and Marriage Therapist and Mental Health Counselor. He is certified as both an elementary and secondary school teacher and holds A.D.E.C. certification as a Death Educator. Dr. Lee is co-chair of the Crime Task Force of the City of Cambridge, Massachusetts, a member of that community's Crisis Response Team, and Commissioner of the Mayor's Commission on Unity and Justice.

LINDA REED MAXWELL was raised in a military family and later married a Naval aviator. She taught elementary education in both public and private schools until the birth of her first child. Mrs. Maxwell's husband was killed in an aircraft accident while deployed to the Mediterranean in 1981, one month after the birth of their second child. This crisis in her life led to an interest in the effects of grief on children. She later wrote a master's thesis on children and death loss (M.Ed., University of North Florida, 1990). During the Gulf War, she was a member of a local crisis intervention team. She has written articles and speaks about military children, the lifestyle they lead, and the losses they face. Recently, she has relocated to Florida due to her second husband's military career.

DAVID K. MEAGHER, ED.D. is a Professor of Health and Nutrition Sciences at Brooklyn College, CUNY where he coordinates the graduate programs in thanatology and gerontology and is editor of *The Thanatology Newsletter*. He is also a past president of the Association of Death Education and Counseling.

MARGARET M. METZGAR is the founder and primary therapist at the *Transition and Loss Center* in Seattle, Washington. She has specialized in dealing with issues of crisis, loss and transition since the mid 1970s. In addition to her private practice, she conducts professional training and workshops and is a well known speaker. Margaret holds a Master's Degree (M.A.) in Therapeutic Psychology from Seattle University and a Bachelor's Degree (B.A.) in Education and Human Services from Western Washington University. She is a certified Paramedic (retired). She is a member of the Association for Death Education and Counseling and the American Counseling Associon. She has published several educator manuals which are available through the Transition and Loss Center, Seattle, Washington.

RICK RITTER is a social worker who has worked as a readjustment counselor in the Veterans Administration Vet Center for eight years. He is co-founder of "Men For Nonviolence," a program for batterers and is a mental health/assessment counselor at Charter Beacon Hospital. He is the lead mental health/CISD officer and mortuary officer for the Allen County Medical Response Team (DMAT Team). He is a stress management instructor and works in private practice with Stress Operations Group. He is engaged in graduate studies in social work at the University of Michigan.

RABBI DANIEL A. ROBERTS is Senior Rabbi at Temple Emanu El in University Heights, Ohio He has lectured extensively on teenage suicide and has produced a video, "Inside I Ache," a trigger film for discussion of teenage suicide in the classroom. Rabbi Roberts has also authored a chapter entitled, "It's Not Over When It's Over: The Aftermath of Suicide" (in *Personal Care in an Impersonal World,* by Dr. Jack Morgan, published by Baywood Publishing), a guide for clergy in helping the family survivors of suicide to mourn.

DIANE RYERSON, A.C.S.W. currently serves as the Director of Consultation and Education for South Bergen Mental Health Center, Inc., Lyndhurst, New Jersey and is President of Peake Ryerson Consulting Group of Englewood, New Jersey. Ms. Ryerson has been a pioneer in the area of school based suicide prevention programming. The Adolescent Suicide Awareness Program (ASAP) has been implemented in over 300 high schools in the United States, Canada, and Western Europe over the past ten years. Ms. Ryerson has authored numerous articles and chapters describing school based prevention programming and is coauthor of American Association of Suicidology School Suicide Postvention Guidelines. Ms. Ryerson serves as a member of the Board of Directors of AAS and has cochaired the School Program Committee since 1985.

EILEEN STEVENSON is a certified school nurse/health educator at Joyce Kilmer School in Mahwah, New Jersey. She is a graduate of St. Vincent's School of Nursing in Worcester, Massachusetts and hold Bachelor's and Master's degrees from Jersey City State College. She is an ADEC certified death educator and has participated in many national and international conferences on death and grief-related themes, such as bereaved children, AIDS, suicide prevention and the school as a support system.

PATRICIA ZALAZNIK is the author of *Dimensions of Loss and Death Education: Curriculum & Resource Guide*. First published in 1979, the third edition was published in 1992. In addition to authoring other related articles, Patricia has taught about loss and death for twenty-two years at the high school level. She has given college and university lectures on the topic as well as at teacher training programs and workshops for professionals and for the general public. Ms. Zalaznik hold national certification as a Death Educator from the Association for Death Education and Counseling, and has an M.A. in education from the University of Minnesota.

Index